FITZGERALD AND THE WAR BETWEEN THE SEXES

BOOKS BY SCOTT DONALDSON

Fitzgerald and the War Between the Sexes

Essays

SCOTT DONALDSON

The Pennsylvania State University Press
University Park, Pennsylvania

Library of Congress Cataloging-in-Publication Data

Names: Donaldson, Scott, 1928–2020, author. | Donaldson, Scott, 1928–2020.
    Tender is the night.
Title: Fitzgerald and the war between the sexes : essays / Scott Donaldson.
Description: University Park, Pennsylvania : The Pennsylvania State University
    Press, [2022] | Includes bibliographical references and index.
Summary: "A collection of five essays on F. Scott Fitzgerald by the biographer
    and critic Scott Donaldson (1928–2020)"—Provided by publisher.
Identifiers: LCCN 2022026217 | ISBN 9780271093956 (hardback) | ISBN
    9780271093963 (paperback)
Subjects: LCSH: Fitzgerald, F. Scott (Francis Scott), 1896–1940—Criticism and
    interpretation. | LCGFT: Essays.
Classification: LCC PS3511.I9 Z5895 2022 | DDC 813/.52—dc23/eng/20220722
LC record available at https://lccn.loc.gov/2022026217

The Pennsylvania State University Press is a member of the Association of
University Presses.

It is the policy of The Pennsylvania State University Press to use acid-free paper.
Publications on uncoated stock satisfy the minimum requirements of American
National Standard for Information Sciences—Permanence of Paper for Printed
Library Material, ANSI Z39.48–1992.

CONTENTS

This collection brings together five essays on F. Scott Fitzgerald by the biographer and critic Scott Donaldson (1928–2020). The first two essays in the collection—"*Tender Is the Night*: The War Between the Sexes" and "Gatsby and the American Dream"—are previously unpublished. "A Fitzgerald Autobiography" (2002) and "Scott and Dottie" (2016) are previously uncollected. "Summer of '24: Zelda's Affair" is reprinted from Scott's book *The Impossible Craft* (2015).

Scott devoted a substantial portion of his career to the study of Fitzgerald's life and works. His fourth book, *Fool for Love* (1983), is one of the best biographies we have of the author; two other books, *Hemingway vs. Fitzgerald* (1999) and *Fitzgerald and Hemingway: Works and Days* (2009), examine the contentious friendship between the two writers and bring together Scott's essays on their lives and careers. He continued to think and write about Fitzgerald's works until the end, taking fresh approaches to the novels and stories and drawing on his knowledge of Fitzgerald's life and writing habits for new insights.

The first and longest of the essays here, "*Tender Is the Night*: The War Between the Sexes," is in effect a short book about one of the central issues in Fitzgerald's last completed novel—the contest between men and women for dominance in a marriage or a relationship. The second piece, "Gatsby and the American Dream," is a perceptive essay about the themes in Fitzgerald's most widely read novel, with special attention to the importance of money and status in American society. The third essay, "Summer of '24: Zelda's Affair," examines Zelda Fitzgerald's romance with Edouard Jozan, the French aviator she met on the Riviera while her husband was composing *The Great Gatsby*. The fourth piece, "Scott and Dottie," tells the story of the friendship and (perhaps) brief affair between Fitzgerald and the writer Dorothy Parker. And the final essay, "A Fitzgerald Autobiography," sets forth suggestions for assembling the memoir that Fitzgerald thought of writing in the late 1930s, in the years shortly before his death.

The pieces in this collection demonstrate Scott's many talents. The essay on *Tender Is the Night* is the best close reading of the novel that I have seen. The interpretation of *The Great Gatsby* is an expansive and illuminating overview of the characters and themes in that novel. The two pieces that follow—on Zelda Fitzgerald and Edouard Jozan, and on Fitzgerald and Dorothy Parker—show Scott as a biographer, marshalling evidence and testimony, assessing their value, and fashioning a narrative from what he has discovered. The fifth essay, on Fitzgerald's never-written autobiography, is speculative and stimulating; it prompts the reader to think about the book we might have today, had Fitzgerald lived long enough to put that book into print.

Scott was an excellent scholar and a good man, generous with his time and knowledge. (See the obituaries in the *Minneapolis Star Tribune*, 6 December 2020, and the *New York Times*, 29 December 2020.) He brought a newspaperman's curiosity to his work and an open, accessible style to his writing. One always felt in good hands when reading a book or an essay by Scott. His prose was clear and direct, with personal touches throughout. He brought the reader along with him in each investigation, following the leads and weighing the evidence. Of his many books, the two I liked best were his biographies of John Cheever and Edwin Arlington Robinson. In writing Cheever's life, Scott overcame obstacles placed in his path by the author's heirs. In the Robinson biography he dealt with a man who lived an unusually quiet life, an artist to whom not very much happened. Scott brought both writers to life, blending their careers with interpretations of their writings, not just of the best-known pieces but of the entire oeuvre of each author.

I admired Scott's commitment to his work after retirement. He took time for bridge and tennis but continued to devote his primary energies to his writing. He was open to new ideas about the authors who interested him. He liked to encourage young scholars who, he knew, would benefit from his example and continue his work. He will be greatly missed in the Fitzgerald field and in American literary scholarship. He was a perceptive critic, an excellent close reader, and a first-rate biographer. He leaves behind a substantial body of work that will continue to inform and influence students, teachers, and scholars.

JAMES L. W. WEST III

SPARKS PROFESSOR OF ENGLISH, EMERITUS

THE PENNSYLVANIA STATE UNIVERSITY

ACKNOWLEDGMENTS

For permission to assemble this volume and assistance with materials and information, I thank Scott's son and literary executor, Brit Donaldson, and his wife, Vivian Donaldson. Thanks also to Kirk Curnutt, Troy State University, coeditor of the *F. Scott Fitzgerald Review*, for locating Scott's essay on *The Great Gatsby*, which Scott wrote as the introduction to a proposed volume of the best criticism, by divers hands, that had been published about the novel. For permission to reprint Scott's previously published writings I am grateful to the *Sewanee Review*, the *F. Scott Fitzgerald Review*, and Penn State University Press.

PREVIOUS APPEARANCES ARE AS FOLLOWS:
"Summer of '24: Zelda's Affair." *The Impossible Craft: Literary Biography*. University Park: Penn State UP, 2015. 173-88.
"Scott and Dottie." First published in the *Sewanee Review* 124, no. 1 (2016): 40-61. Reprinted with permission of the author's literary estate and the editor.
"A Fitzgerald Autobiography." *F. Scott Fitzgerald Review* 1 (2002): 143-57.

For three of the pieces in the collection I have preserved the style of documentation from the original. These are *"Tender Is the Night*: The War Between the Sexes," "Summer of '24: Zelda's Affair," and "A Fitzgerald Autobiography." The other two essays, "Gatsby and the American Dream" and "Scott and Dottie," are general treatments which the author wrote without formal documentation.

J. L. W. W. III

ABBREVIATIONS

EH   Ernest Hemingway
FSF   F. Scott Fitzgerald
MJB   Matthew J. Bruccoli
SD   Scott Donaldson

ONE

Tender Is the Night

The War Between the Sexes

The war is over and I scarcely knew there was a war . . .

—LETTER, PSYCHIATRIC PATIENT NICOLE WARREN TO US ARMY
CAPTAIN DR. RICHARD DIVER, NOVEMBER 1918 (FSF, *TENDER* 114)

I. WAR AND ITS PRACTITIONERS

War qualified as "the best subject of all" for fiction, Ernest Hemingway wrote his new friend F. Scott Fitzgerald on 15 December 1925, and he understood why Fitzgerald was "sore" that he'd "missed" the war, lamenting in "I Didn't Get Over" (1936) and elsewhere that he had not fought on the World War I battlefields (EH, *Letters* 446). Despite that handicap, Fitzgerald wrote a great novel about war: *Tender Is the Night.* The conflict he powerfully depicted in that book concentrated on the struggle for dominance, the battle, the war between the sexes—a kind of warfare he hadn't missed at all and was deeply involved in. Throughout his book he presented that conflict in the context of wars between nations, repeatedly drawing connections between the battlefield and the home front.

It took Fitzgerald nine long years, and several false starts, to finish *Tender Is the Night.* He began the book shortly after *The Great Gatsby* was published in the spring of 1925 and did not complete it until mid-1934. By February

1928, although he had yet to make much progress on his novel, he was manifestly obsessed by the Great War. He and Zelda were then living at Ellerslie, an estate outside Wilmington, Delaware, and had invited a number of friends to a weekend house party. During a pause in the carousing, Fitzgerald read a chapter from his work in progress to Edmund Wilson and Gilbert Seldes. Wilson knew better than to ask when the book would be ready for publication—any inquiry along those lines, he had found, would elicit "a sharp retort" from Fitzgerald. What most struck Wilson that weekend was his Princeton friend Fitzgerald's interest in World War I. In inviting Wilson to the party he'd referred to the "slaughter of Paschendale [*sic*]" and the troops' "shivering in the lagoons at Ypres." In Fitzgerald's study at Ellerslie, he'd hung on the wall the unused trench helmet he'd been issued during the war. And he showed Wilson an album of photographs he'd assembled of soldiers mutilated in combat (Wilson).

What was all that about? Wilson wondered. He got his answer six years later, when *Tender Is the Night* finally came out. It is a book saturated with references to and commentary on warfare. As Fitzgerald told his editor Max Perkins while writing his novel, "the whole motif" of his novel was "taken from Ludendorff's memoirs": more specifically the passage in which German general Erich Ludendorff laments the failure of his 1918 spring offensive with the remark that "the song of the frogs on the river drowned the rumble of our artillery." So in *Tender*, Perkins concluded, "there was all this lovely veneer, and rottenness and horror underneath" (MJB, *Composition* xi).

The most explicit linking of war between the sexes and between nations emerges in Dr. Richard Diver's conversation with "the woman in room twenty," one of his most troubled patients. An American painter who had lived in Paris for some time, she became "all mad and gone" and was consigned to treatment at the Swiss clinic on the Zugersee jointly run by Doctors Diver and Gregorovious.

This woman, exceptionally pretty on arrival at the clinic, is beset by a terrible eczema that transforms her into "a living agonizing sore." The area about her eyes becomes so swollen that she cannot see Diver when he comes to counsel her. She is very much his particular patient, for he is the only doctor who can offer her even temporary relief, and over time he "comes to love" her. Yet nothing he does can restore her to health. At the end Diver stays up with her three nights in a row, trying to forestall the darkness ahead, but then she dies, leaving him exhausted and devastated.

Aware that Zelda Fitzgerald suffered badly from eczema during her confinement in Swiss mental institutions, many readers believe that Fitzgerald based this "scabbed anonymous woman-artist" with a deep thrilling voice on his own wife. And surely, the dialogue between doctor and patient reflects what Fitzgerald, at the time he was writing the last version of his novel, regarded as a contest between himself and Zelda that would leave the loser vanquished, defeated, done.

Her eczema is a nervous phenomenon, Diver tells his patient, but she attributes her illness to another, more generalized cause.

"I'm sharing the fate of the women of my time who challenged men to battle," she declares.

"To your vast surprise it was just like all battles," he replies, prompting her to elaborate on the metaphor. "Just like all battles. . . . You pick a set-up, or else win a Pyrrhic victory, or you're wrecked and ruined," she says. Diver denies that she has been either wrecked or ruined. "Look at me!" she furiously demands.

"You've suffered," Diver acknowledges, "but many women suffered before they mistook themselves for men." And in any case, she should not confuse her present condition with a final defeat. She is not persuaded by his rationale, and privately, to be sure, Diver thinks that she is too finespun to win her battle, that it's "too tough a game" for her.

That unspoken diagnosis proves to be accurate: she cannot compete successfully against men on the harrowing "frontiers of [artistic] consciousness" and succumbs (209-12, 273). It is highly significant, however, that she is the only woman who *loses* in the modern war between the sexes delineated throughout *Tender Is the Night*. Otherwise, the women win.

This is true not only, most notably, of Nicole Warren Diver, whose triumph over her doctor-husband is dramatized in a series of excruciating scenes throughout Book Three of the novel, but also in the portrayals of Rosemary Hoyt; her mother, Elsie Speers; the Divers' friend Mary North Minghetti; and Nicole's sister Baby Warren.

Rosemary's Angle
Tender Is the Night begins with Rosemary Hoyt on Gausse's beach, not quite eighteen years old but already a movie star in *Daddy's Girl*, a title fraught with meaning for Fitzgerald's narrative. With the dew still on her, she is absolutely

adorable. Her palms are magically pink, her cheeks lit to a lovely flame, her eyes "bright, big, clear, wet, and shining." Ash blonde and golden hair covers her head—and here, as often in passages about women, the author introduces a military comparison—"like an armorial shield." This metaphor is developed in the description of her mother, Elsie Speers: twice married—to a cavalry officer and an army doctor—and twice widowed, she brings up her daughter to be "hard," so that Rosemary is "protected by a double sheath of her mother's armor and her own" (9-10, 19).

Young as she is, Rosemary understands the value of her sex appeal. She is dispatched by her mother to visit film director Earl Brady in Monte Carlo, and as Brady looks her over "from head to foot," she welcomes his calculating appraisal: "If her person was property she could exercise whatever advantage was inherent in its ownership" (30). But it was different with Dick Diver.

Book One of the novel is related primarily from Rosemary's point of view, and almost at first glance she falls in love with Diver, twice her age at thirty-four, and married for more than five years to the beautiful and mentally disturbed Nicole. Dick comes by, her first day on the beach, to warn Rosemary against sunburn. Two mornings later, he asks her to join his group, which includes himself and Nicole (and their children), Abe and Mary North, and Tommy Barban. "We go in, we take food and drink, so it's a substantial invitation," he declares, and of course she accepts, for Dick strikes her as kind and charming, and very much in charge, organizing each day for the most agreeable outcome. She has the sense, too, that he "was taking care of her, and she delighted in responding" to the day's well-planned movement "as if it had been an order" (23, 28).

At that first lunch with the Divers, Rosemary compares Dick favorably to Abe and Tommy, characters who function in the novel as contrasts with the protagonist. Unlike the other men, Dick seems "all complete" to her, with his reddish hair and complexion, his bright blue eyes, the hardness and self-discipline she senses in him, and his voice with a faint Irish lilt that woos the world in comments suggesting more than they say. "Oh, she chose him," but Nicole sees her do so (26), and though as Rosemary will soon tell her mother she is desperately in love with Dick, she likes Nicole, too, and the situation seems hopeless.

Elsie Speers, no ordinary stage mother, responds that Rosemary ought to be happy to be in love and encourages her to pursue the relationship. "[G]o ahead and put whatever happens down to experience . . . it can't spoil you because economically you're a boy, not a girl" (29, 49).

So Rosemary Hoyt sets out to attract Dick Diver, repeatedly telling him that she's fallen in love with him. He answers her declarations of love with ambiguous but hardly off-putting remarks. "New friends can often have a better time together than old friends," he says, and later, "You have romantic eyes" (39, 47). Eventually her boldness has its reward, for Dick has always been susceptible to the attractions of young girls who "actually look like something blooming" (29). With the Riviera season coming to an end, he invites Rosemary to accompany Nicole and himself and the Norths on their return to Paris. There, in a series of episodes near the end of Book One, Dick and Rosemary shift positions in the contest for dominance that foreshadows the similar experience of Dick and Nicole in Books Two and Three.

As Milton Stern and David Rennie have noted, references to World War I permeate Fitzgerald's novels, and *Tender Is the Night* in particular. Admittedly, Diver's service in the war did not put him at risk. Too valuable as a Rhodes Scholar and physician "to be shot off in a gun" (133), he is assigned to counseling work far removed from combat zones. The war hasn't touched him at all, he maintains. Yet he is portrayed in connection with military figures throughout *Tender Is the Night*. When his coterie, resettled in Paris, decides to visit the battlefield at Beaumont-Hamel, he plays the role of expert. He prepares for the day only by making "a quick study" (70) of the guidebooks but manages to carry it off anyway, for Dick is a consummate performer. Later, Rosemary attempts to arrange a screen test for him and comments, "Oh, we're such *actors*—you and I" (121).

The basic point of Diver's discourse at Beaumont-Hamel is that the Great War marked the bloody end of long-held attachments to nationalist ideals. Addressing himself primarily to Rosemary, who is prepared to accept and admire anything he says—"[y]ou know everything," she remarks—Dick points out that the bare green land before them "cost twenty lives a foot" in the summer of 1916 and that such terrible carnage could not be repeated for a long time. This "western-front business," he maintains, required "religion and years of plenty and tremendous sureties and the exact relation that existed between the classes." To fight and die in such a battle, you had to have "a whole-souled sentimental equipment" based on memories of "Christmas . . . and little cafes in Valence and beer gardens in Unter den Linden and weddings at the mairie, and going to the Derby, and your grandfather's whiskers" (75).

Abe North, who unlike Dick had seen battle service in the war, tries to bring his friend's rhetoric down to earth. In the course of doing so, Abe cites two men who figure prominently in interpretations of Fitzgerald's novel. General Ulysses S. Grant invented a similar kind of battle at Petersburg in 1865, Abe maintains. Not so, Dick answers—Grant "just invented mass butchery." And in objecting to Dick's assertion that this was "the last love battle," Abe remarks that Dick "want[s] to hand over this battle to D. H. Lawrence" (67-69). The reference to Lawrence reflects the combative nature of relations between the sexes both in Lawrence's writing and in his life. In the spring of 1930, Fitzgerald read Lawrence's *Fantasia of the Unconscious*, a psychological treatise arguing that the contemporary male's "disinterested craving" to make something wonderful out of himself was undermined by sexual desire and by trying to please the modern female, and as a consequence she had become "the fearless . . . determined positive party . . . a queen of the earth, and inwardly a fearsome tyrant" (SD, "History" 186). Lawrence's argument spoke to Fitzgerald's increasing conviction, during the early 1930s, that he and his wife were engaged in a struggle for survival. He wrote that struggle into *Tender Is the Night*.

The reference to Grant, like several others in the novel, emphasizes the parallel between his career and that of Diver. Twice the novel calls attention to the humiliating years Grant spent clerking in his family's store in Galena, Illinois—it's also mentioned in *The Great Gatsby*—after being forced to resign his Army commission for excessive drinking (*Tender* 136, 352, 375; *Gatsby* 43, 170). Interestingly, Fitzgerald's maternal grandfather, Philip F. McQuillan, an Irish immigrant who made a small fortune in the wholesale grocery business, came upstream on the Mississippi from Galena to St. Paul. When the Civil War broke out, of course, Grant was called back to the service and rapidly rose to become commanding general of the Union armies and, eventually, president of the United States. In the last sentence of the book, Nicole allows herself to think that Dick Diver, the husband and doctor she has cast aside and who has his own problems with alcohol, might somehow *not* be lapsing into obscurity somewhere in the Finger Lakes section of New York. Perhaps, she speculates, "his career was biding its time . . . like Grant's in Galena" (352).

The battlefield scene immediately precedes a demonstration of Diver's authority and charm. He reassures "a red-haired girl from Tennessee" who has come to lay a wreath on her brother's grave but cannot locate it among so many others. Just place the wreath on any grave, Dick suggests; that's what her brother would have wanted her to do (69). It's a small matter, but illustrative of Diver's pervasive eagerness to put himself out for the benefit of those around him. "He sometimes looked back with awe at the carnivals of affection he had given," Fitzgerald writes, "as a general might gaze upon a massacre he had ordered to satisfy an impersonal blood lust" (35).

The novel's military theme persists in two comic scenes involving generals. Back in Paris, Diver asserts over lunch at Voisins that he is the only American man with "repose." (Incidentally, John Irwin points out that in 1934, after reading *Tender*, Cole Porter modified the lyrics of "You're the Top" from "You're a rose" to "You're repose" [Irwin 34-38].) Abe North takes exception to Diver's claim, and the others watch eagerly for an example to contradict it. But every American man who enters the restaurant, conscious that he's being observed, fails the test for repose by raising a hand to his face: to finger his eyeglasses, adjust his tie, pat his cheek, and so on. Then "a well-known general" comes in, and Abe, knowing of the ramrod training at West Point, makes a five-dollar bet with Dick that the general will prove the exception to Diver's rule. The West Pointer keeps his hands down, and it looks as if Abe will win the bet, but at the last minute, with lunch over, the waiter pulls out the general's chair, and "[w]ith a touch of fury the conqueror shot up his hand and scratched his gray immaculate head" (62-63).

Diver is right about *his* repose, at least at this juncture, and Rosemary is duly impressed. Back in Paris, she couches his mastery of social situations in imagery borrowed from warfare. At one of his parties, Rosemary admires Dick's "technic of moving many varied types, each as immobile, as dependent on supplies of attention as an infantry battalion is dependent on rations," and accomplishing these maneuvers so effortlessly that "he still had pieces of his own most personal self for everyone." That last clause, though, clashes with the fleeting thought Fitzgerald puts into her mind. "When people have so much for outsiders didn't it indicate a lack of inner intensity?" (90, 87).

That idea presumably occurs to Rosemary even as she attempts, for her eighteenth birthday present, to have Dick make love to her. Earlier that evening they have been together and have kissed for the first time. Once in her room, she presses against him and whispers, "Take me." It is "one of her greatest rôles," Rosemary understands, and she passionately throws herself into it. "Go on," she pleads. "I want you to do it now, take me, show me, I'm absolutely yours and I want to be." Dick backs away. What about Nicole? he asks, and leaves the room. Rosemary is devastated, but only for the time being. When she sees him the next day, "their eyes [meet] and [brush] like birds' wings" and she is wildly happy and full of confidence, sure that he is beginning to fall in love with her (74-79). The dynamic between them has begun to change.

Walking a few steps behind him that afternoon, Rosemary continues to admire and adore Dick as "organizer of private gaiety, curator of a richly incrusted happiness," handsomely turned out with his perfect hat, yellow gloves, and heavy stick. She thinks "what a good time they would all have being with him" that night, and indeed they do, for Dick orchestrates one of his most memorable parties, guiding them on a quick odyssey around Paris. The group grows and shrinks as planned, expert authorities appearing and vanishing as needed, everything foreseen, including a ride in the fabulous car of the shah of Persia. Never has Rosemary known anyone "so thoroughly nice" as Dick was that night. They dance together, and she "feels her beauty sparkling bright against his tall, strong form" (89-90).

The climax—the second comic scene involving a general—comes during the early morning hours when half a dozen of the partygoers invade the lobby of the Ritz, telling the hotel's night concierge that General Pershing, commander of the American Expeditionary Forces, waits outside, wants caviar and champagne, and will brook no delay. Frantic activity ensues, waiters emerging from nowhere to set up a table in the lobby. Then Abe North arrives in an unconvincing portrayal of Black Jack Pershing as his companions mumble fragments of war songs for his benefit. The disillusioned waiters leave, prompting the Diver group to "build a waiter trap" by rearranging the lobby furniture. Or, as Abe repeatedly proposes, they might open up a waiter with a musical saw to discover what's inside.

The Divers go home after the Ritz lobby fiasco, and Dick tries to talk Rosemary into coming with them. Ordinarily she would have agreed, but, she explains, she has promised Mary North to try to persuade Abe to go to bed. At eleven that very morning, Abe is scheduled to catch the boat train on his way to the United States, where—Mary desperately hopes—he will be able to resume his career as a musician and composer. Rosemary wants to help, if possible.

"Don't you know you can't do anything about people?" Dick brusquely objects, in a comment belying his occupation. If Abe had been his roommate in college, "tight for the first time," he tells Rosemary, it might be different. He likes and even loves Abe North, but he knows that his friend is too far gone in alcoholism to recover (91). There is irony building here, for the parallel declines of Dick and Abe become unmistakably clear as the novel progresses.

Turning Point

Book One ends with a series of deadly encounters, underscoring the novel's theme of martial violence and Dick Diver's fading command of romantic relationships. The most significant of these incidents occurs at the Gare St. Lazare the morning after the odyssey around Paris. In half a dozen pages—coming less than one third of the way through the narrative—Dick cedes a significant measure of control both to his wife, Nicole, and to his putative lover, Rosemary. This marks a basic turning point in *Tender Is the Night*.

Nicole arrives at the train station in advance of the others to bid farewell to Abe North. Abe has been "heavy . . . in love" with Nicole for years and she likes him better than anyone except her husband, we are told, but there is little to like about this depiction of Abe, who is badly hung over that morning and disillusioned with himself, everyone else, and life itself. Nicole begins with small talk, but Abe responds with a series of insults and unpleasantries: "I'm tired of you both"; "Tired of women's worlds"; "Tired of friends. The thing is to have sycophants" (93-95). This last "tired" phrase about friends and sycophants was one Fitzgerald particularly liked: it appeared half a dozen times in various versions of the *Tender* manuscript, and the idea is elaborated further in "The Crack-Up" (1936).

Fitzgerald interrupts this dialogue with one of his telling comments on the sexes: "Often a man can play the helpless child in front of a woman, but he can almost never bring it off when he feels most like a helpless child." So it is as Nicole slaps back at Abe, "a rough nap on [her] velvet gloves" (94).

Early in the story, Nicole is described as "hard and lovely and pitiful," a trio of adjectives that sum up her presence (12). Her loveliness is beyond dispute, outshining Rosemary's as a painting by Leonardo da Vinci surpasses the work of a professional illustrator. And as the victim of an incestuous father, she surely deserves pity. But "hard" seems contradictory at first. Rosemary does reflect, on the beach one day, that she would not like to have Nicole for an enemy and comes to regard her as a force to be reckoned with. Yet Nicole's hardness—which will by Book Three develop into Georgia pine, the hardest wood known except for New Zealand lignum vitae (309)—is not firmly demonstrated, not *shown*, in the novel until the scene with the despondent

Abe North at the Gare St. Lazare. There, with an assertiveness that surprises even herself, she forcefully criticizes him in this interchange:

> "I am a woman and my business is to hold things together."
> "My business is to tear them apart."
> "When you get drunk you don't tear anything apart except yourself."

In that last, frighteningly direct criticism, Nicole confronts Abe with the source of his worst problems—his defeatism, his exhaustion, his "giv[ing] up about everything," including friends (94-95).

It is precisely at this point that a "tall girl with straw hair like a helmet" comes into view at the station. This is Maria Wallis, a member of the American community in Paris who is about to commit, literally, the crime that Fitzgerald's novel figuratively embodies. Nicole rushes off to greet her and to escape Abe but is unaccountably snubbed. "Let people come to you," she remarks afterward: the comment of someone absolutely sure of her social position (95).

Rosemary and Mary North then arrive, followed by Dick Diver, and all three women spring "like monkeys" onto his shoulders as Dick enables them, at least for a moment, to ignore the "gigantic obscenity" of Abe's "survivant will"—once a will to live, now a will to die (96). Abe boards the train, but then, on the platform two Pullman cars away—it is Nicole who sees it— the helmet-haired Maria Wallis plunges her hand into her purse, retrieves a small pearl-handled revolver, and fires twice at an Englishman (presumably her lover, about to leave her on the boat train), wounding but not killing him and penetrating his "identification card."

Dick fights his way through the crowd to find out these details, and returns, five minutes later, with a plan of action. He has discovered which police station they are taking Maria Wallis to, and he will go there, he announces, to make sure that they don't do "anything outrageous" to her. But Nicole, emboldened by her confrontation with Abe, scotches that plan. "Wait!" she commands Dick. Maria's sister Laura lives in Paris, married to a Frenchman, and it would be better to phone her with the news. They could do more than anyone else, and besides, what good could Dick do "with [his] French"? Dick is unconvinced—and "also he was showing off for Rosemary." But Nicole once again firmly directs him, "[y]ou wait," and hurries off to make the necessary phone call. She takes charge of the situation, while Dick, her doctor and husband, can only remark that once "Nicole takes things into her hands there is nothing more to be done."

While Nicole is away on her errand, Dick and Rosemary exchange glances, and the "slow warm hum of love" begins again, but now, Dick realizes for the first time, Rosemary "ha[s] her hand on the lever more authoritatively than he." And when Nicole returns, having completed her mission, both she and Rosemary—despite being accustomed in the movies "to having shell fragments of such events shriek past her head"—wait in vain for Dick "to make a moral comment on the matter." Dr. Diver, shaken by his loss of emotional control, cannot manage to summon such a comment. They leave the station "as if nothing had happened," but, Fitzgerald reminds us, "[e]verything had."

It remains for two French porters, in a chapter-ending conversation, to link Maria Wallis's shooting of the Englishman to the novel's dominant theme. Her revolver, one of them observes, was very small, like a toy. But powerful enough, the other answers, to cause "so much blood you'd think it was the war" (96-99).

≈

Fact intersected with fiction in Fitzgerald's account of this shooting. On 26 March 1927, Countess Alice de Janzé, née Alice Silverthorne of Chicago, a cousin of J. Ogden Armour and well known in American (and French) social circles, shot her lover Raymund de Trafford and herself at the Gare du Nord. At the time Alice was estranged from her French husband, Frédéric, because of her affair with de Trafford, scion of a prominent English family. But de Trafford was planning to leave her, departing on the boat train to Boulogne, and she could not abide that. So she purchased a small 3.8-caliber Colt revolver with a pearl handle, and after a farewell luncheon with de Trafford, she accompanied him to his first-class compartment, where she opened fire in an attempted murder-suicide. Both of them were seriously wounded but survived. The news was widely reported in newspapers at the time, where Fitzgerald saw it and wrote it into his book-in-progress.

The details of this event are described in Paul Spicer's 2010 book *The Temptress*, which goes on to cite Alice's subsequent scandalous and possibly murderous behavior among the wealthy "Happy Valley" set in Kenya (Spicer).

≈

Another pearl-handled revolver surfaces in the "Wanda Breasted" episode, an outtake from an early draft of *Tender Is the Night* printed as an appendix to the 1951 version of the novel edited by Malcolm Cowley. That edition, following instructions Fitzgerald left behind, tells the story chronologically rather than beginning with Rosemary's worshipful portrait of Dick Diver in the mid-1920s before segueing back to his romance with and eventual marriage to Nicole Warren following the end of World War I. According to Cowley, Fitzgerald sacrificed a brilliant beginning by advocating such a revision, but more than made up for it by making it clear that the novel is psychological, that it is about Dick Diver.

The sacrifice, subsequent readers and editors decided, was not worth making, and the 1951 edition did not succeed in replacing the novel as published in 1934. In proposing the reorganization of *Tender*, Fitzgerald was influenced by reviewers who criticized the book for its apparently "incoherent" structure and for not adequately preparing, in Book One, for Dick's eventual failure. But there were early clues that Diver was ill equipped to win his battles of the sexes, culminating in the climactic Gare St. Lazare scene. From that stage on, Fitzgerald presents a series of events testifying to Diver's present and future collapse. He is charming, but exerts his charm as a way of satisfying his need for the love and approval of others. He is overly susceptible to the appeal of vibrant young girls like Rosemary and inordinately jealous of any rivals. His dignity is compromised by his giving in to the inducements of too much Warren wealth. Like Abe before him, he turns to drink as his emotions begin to roil.

And he does not even realize, at first, what is happening. Fitzgerald as narrator intrudes after the Maria Wallis shooting to sum up the situation. "Dick had no suspicion of the sharpness of the change; he was profoundly unhappy and the subsequent increase of egotism tended momentarily to blind him to what was going on round about him" (100).

A great deal goes on during the rest of that day, nearly all of it demeaning for Diver. Collis Clay, the young Yale man besotted with Rosemary Hoyt, arrives for lunch in the Luxembourg Gardens too late to see her, and Dick uncharacteristically stays with him, finishing the last of the wine and letting the early afternoon hours escape as Collis tells him about an apparent sexual indiscretion of Rosemary's during a train trip. Dick's jealousy takes over to construct an imagined dialogue in the compartment of the boy she thought was "pretty nutsey" at the time.

—The boy: "Do you mind if I pull down the curtain?"
—Rosemary: "Please do. It's too light in here." (102)

Once this exchange enters his mind, Dick cannot shake loose of it. "Do you mind if I pull down the curtain?" comes back to disturb him five more times (103, 104, 108, 116, 192).

Next, Diver stops by his bank to collect his mail and cash a check on Nicole's account. This could cause embarrassment, and Dick carefully considers which teller he should approach: not Muchhause, certainly, "who always asked him whether he wanted to draw upon his wife's money or his own," but perhaps Pierce or Perrin or Casasus. He settles on Casasus as the one for whom he would have to put on the least self-protective performance. It is a brilliant scene, one that demeans Diver even as he manages to avoid an overt public wound to his psyche (103-4). Fitzgerald's friend Robert Benchley, reading *Tender Is the Night* two weeks after publication, commented that as "a journeyman writer" himself he could not even imagine being able "to do that scene in the Guaranty Trust." Benchley also intuited that Fitzgerald was, at least in part, writing out of his own distress in his new novel. "I hope that you, yourself," he wrote Fitzgerald on 29 April 1934, "are not any unhappier than is called for in the general blueprint specifications for living." Anyone capable of crawling around all afternoon to play tin soldiers with a bunch of kids—as Benchley had seen Scott do at the Murphys' home in Antibes—didn't deserve to be unhappy (Benchley to FSF, 29 April 1934).

Upon leaving the bank Diver takes a taxi to Passy, where, he knows, Rosemary is to visit the Films Par Excellence Studio. But they have made no arrangements to meet, so Diver walks around the block, hoping to catch sight of the actress as she leaves the studio—a foolish and futile endeavor more in character for one of Booth Tarkington's fatuous adolescents (Penrod, perhaps) than for the perfectly turned out Dr. Diver. But he is tortured by jealousy and unable to conduct himself with dignity. Having missed connections with Rosemary, he calls her hotel room to confess that he's "in an extraordinary condition" about her. Then this exchange:

"Are you alone?"
—*Do you mind if I pull down the curtain?*
"Who do you think I'd be with?"

In fact, he has good reason to be jealous, for, as Rosemary writes her mother, at the studio in Passy she has met the man who will direct her next film, thinks him wonderful looking, has fallen in love with him. "(Of course I Do Love Dick Best but you know what I mean)." From this time on, Rosemary has the leverage to rule their romance (106-9).

Abe North, it turns out, has not yet gone back to the United States, and he returns, sodden with drink, to involve everyone in the chaotic and deadly conclusion to Book One: the murder of the Afro-European Jules Peterson. "This seems to be the open season" for killings, Dick remarks, as he maneuvers, using his marital financial clout, to extricate Rosemary, Nicole, and himself from any connection with the crime (126-29).

One morning, the three of them discuss the cause of Abe's alcoholism. Why does he have to drink? Rosemary asks. Lots of smart men "go to pieces nowadays," the Divers agree by way of an answer, but Nicole objects to Dick's generalization that this is because they "play close to the line" and "some of them can't stand it." "Why is it just Americans who dissipate?" she demands.

Again, as she had at the train station, Nicole has the last word, and the narrator invades Dick's consciousness to elaborate on the change. Diver regards his wife as "the most attractive human being he has ever seen," yet at the same time he has begun to scent "battle from afar" with her and has been hardening and arming himself "subconsciously" (114-15).

It's a struggle, a battle, a war that will play out in a postwar world lacking the traditional standards of the one Diver grew up in. At lunch following their talk about Abe, the Divers and Rosemary are seated next to a group of American women neither young nor old, nor of any particular social class, yet manifestly bound together as more of a unit than any ordinary tourists. These, a waiter explains, "are the gold-star muzzers," those who lost a son or a husband in the war. In Dick's eyes, these women make the room beautiful. In their dignity, and their happy faces, he sees "all the maturity of an older America," one he'd temporarily inhabited as a boy on his father's knee, entranced by tales of the "Gray Ghost" John Singleton Mosby and his Rangers, irregular Confederate troops who harassed Union forces with lightning night attacks and escaped retaliation by simply fading away afterward (115-16).

This passage links the Gold Star mothers and Diver's father as representative of a better, sounder, and less materialistic period than the one developing in the wake of the Great War. As David Brown observed in his *Paradise Lost*, Fitzgerald's major fiction invariably carries the stamp of "a cultural historian"

(Brown 1). Not only do his novels—and *Tender Is the Night,* above all—accurately represent the customs and manners of the times he was writing about. They also convey his conviction that the romantic idealism bequeathed to him by his father—there is little differentiation between Fitzgerald's father and Diver's in the novel—was giving way to the corruption of a society in which money ruled as supremely powerful. In his excellent 1994 book, Milton Stern calls *Tender "the* American historical novel" (Stern, *Broken* 4, 12).

Several years later Diver crosses the Atlantic to attend his father's funeral. "Good-bye, my father—good-bye, all my fathers," he says by way of farewell, for in the death of his father he intuits the passing of a time when "nothing could be superior to 'good instincts,' honor, courtesy, and courage" (232-33). Shorn of that stabilizing heritage and his father's moral guidance, Diver returns from the funeral to the disastrous secret reunion with Rosemary in Rome and the inebriated aftermath that lands him, badly beaten, in jail.

Tommy Barban as Warrior

Tommy Barban, mercenary soldier, stands in opposition to such admirable figures as Diver's father and the Gold Star mothers. Half French and half American, and educated in England, Barban—whose name reads like an abbreviated version of "barbarian"—welcomes wars and is willing to fight in them if adequately compensated, never mind on which side. He explains his behavior to Rosemary at the "really *bad* party" (35) the Divers give at their Villa Diana in Tarmes. Tommy will leave in the morning, not to go home— he has no home—but to go to war. Any war will do. He doesn't care what he's fighting for, he tells Rosemary, "so long as he's well-treated." In pursuit of this profession, he's "worn the uniforms of eight countries." He likes the Divers—"especially her"—but after a few weeks with them he's ready to go to war again (38).

Rosemary Hoyt is understandably put off by Tommy's matter-of-fact comments about his profession, but the Divers' exquisite consideration of every guest at the dinner table restores her sense of pleasure in the evening, and she decides she likes everyone, including Tommy, with the exception of Albert McKisco, the pretentious novelist-in-process. McKisco tries to start arguments with Dick Diver and Abe North, who do not respond to his insulting overtures, but on the strength of too much champagne McKisco finally succeeds in challenging Barban into a political exchange. "Why do you want to fight the Soviets?" McKisco demands. He himself is not a Communist, he explains, but a Socialist who supports the Russian revolution. "Well," Barban answers, "I'm a soldier. My business is to kill people." And he has fought the Communists because they want to take his property (43). The effects of the Soviet experiment resonate in the novel, in glimpses of White Russian exiles reduced to menial tasks on the Riviera and, most notably, midway through Book Two, in the account of Tommy's bloodily enabling the escape of Prince Chillicheff.

McKisco and Barban have already engaged in this adversarial dialogue when Violet McKisco returns from her visit to the bathroom, where she has presumably observed Nicole in a painfully vivid display of mental illness. Violet is about to tell the others what she's seen when Tommy rises and declares, "It's inadvisable to comment on what goes on in this house." That might have ended the conflict, but during the ride down to Gausse's hotel Violet once again brings up what she had seen (we never know precisely what it was) of Nicole at her most vulnerable, and Tommy once again objects. At first his objection is polite and formal: "Mrs. McKisco, please don't talk further about Mrs. Diver." But when Violet persists and her husband rises to her defense, Barban explodes against McKisco with a fierce cry of anger, in a voice for cavalry: *"You've got to shut up and shut your wife up!"* McKisco announces that he is not afraid of Barban and that they ought to have "the code duello" in operation. This is a mistake, for Barban travels with a set of dueling pistols and at once slaps McKisco as an insult demanding settlement in a duel.

The fight is between two men, as Abe North observes, but it is noteworthy that both of them are motivated by women to risk death or injury in the duel, Tommy Barban to defend Nicole's honor, and McKisco to defend Violet's, who he knows would "never respect him again" had he backed down (44, 52-55). McKisco survives the duel, with the aid of Abe as his second and the Dutch courage of drink, and only appears once again in the course of the novel. Barban goes off to his war, later to become a crucially important figure.

The most telling depiction of Tommy Barban occurs in Munich, where Dick has gone on a "leave of abstinence" (his colleague Franz's locution) from the clinic (221). There, in a Marienplatz café with the air full of politics, "Tommy Barban was a ruler, Tommy was a hero." He has helped Prince Chillicheff, an unsavory Russian aristocrat with "dead yellow eyes," escape from the Soviets. Between them they killed three Red Guards at the border—two for Tommy, one for the prince. The conversation at the café, involving two other Americans, reveals the death of another man in New York: Abe North, who was brutally beaten in a speakeasy and crawled home to the Racquet Club—or the Harvard Club—to die. Unnerved by this news, Diver hardly notices when Barban reveals his plan to change his profession from warrior to stockbroker. Everyone is making millions in the market, Tommy maintains, and he too plans to make a killing that way. The war persists, however, for Diver awakens from a deep sleep to see a long column of German veterans in uniform, marching mournfully to place wreaths on the graves of their fallen comrades (224-28).

≈

Again, as with the case of Maria Wallis, the manner of Abe North's death may well have been borrowed from fact. In a letter to Fitzgerald praising the accomplishment of *Tender Is the Night,"* the famous publisher Bennett Cerf noted that a "chap named Winant" died at the Princeton Club after a speakeasy brawl. According to the 4 May 1928 *New York Times* story, this was Cornelius R. Winant, Princeton '18, so it is likely, as Matthew J. Bruccoli pointed out, that Fitzgerald, as a member of both Princeton '17 and '18, knew Winant during their college days. Also, in his 1931 essay "Echoes of the Jazz Age," Fitzgerald writes of an alcoholic friend "killed in a speakeasy in Chicago" (MJB, "Cerf's Fan Letter" 230; FSF, *My Lost City* 136).

≈

II. THE SEDUCTION OF DR. DIVER

Book Two of *Tender Is the Night* begins in 1919 with a short biography of Dick Diver and moves on to a vivid depiction of his romantic involvement with Nicole Warren, who is then undergoing treatment for mental illness at Dr. Dohmler's clinic near Zurich. A highly talented youth, Diver has been disadvantaged by having too many things go right for him. "Lucky Dick," he was called at Yale, where—for example—he was chosen for an exclusive senior society because another candidate could not be located on Tap Day. It would have been better had he suffered "a little misfortune" and so escaped the illusions that people were essentially good and that he himself was blessed with "eternal strength and health."

In the spring of 1919, Diver is twenty-seven years old and at the peak of his powers. He has studied at Oxford as a Rhodes Scholar, completed his formal training with a medical degree from Johns Hopkins, and spent a productive year in Freud's Vienna working toward his first book. He has returned from noncombatant service in the war to work with his Swiss friend Franz Grego-rovious at Dohmler's clinic. The war hasn't affected him at all, Diver maintains, but his dreams, repeatedly disturbed by martial scenes, belie that assertion. He possesses two remarkable gifts as he launches his professional career: a memory that retains everything he has read, so that he can burn notes and books to heat his spartan quarters, and an extraordinary capacity to charm other people.

Halfway along the tortuous journey from *The Great Gatsby* to *Tender Is the Night*, Fitzgerald wrote that he'd spent almost five years on a novel dealing with "the insoluble problems of personal charm." He had in mind his central character, who began as a model of Gerald Murphy and changed into a psy-chiatrist with a compulsion for pleasing others at prohibitive cost to himself (101).

Dr. Diver cannot help exercising his charm. He wants to be wise and kind and brave, and, rather immodestly, to be "a good psychologist—maybe . . . the greatest one that ever lived" (151), but above all he wants to be loved. He needs the admiration—the love—of others to validate his existence, and he exerts his charm in order to earn it. It is the source of his extraordinary appeal, and his greatest weakness.

In his way Diver resembles another Rhodes Scholar from Yale, one who served as president of the United States and was impeached because of the reckless exercise of his appeal. In his review of Robert Reich's 1997 memoir, *Locked in the Cabinet*, Louis Menand suggests how demeaning it can be to fall under the influence of such a person. Reich served as William Jefferson Clinton's secretary of labor, and his book is not much concerned with poli-tics, Menand points out. It's about Reich's relationship with Clinton.

> [It is] the story of the intelligent, capable person who becomes friends with someone who is no more intelligent or capable, but who is blessed with a power of charm or social facility that cannot be learned or imi-tated. When the charm is turned on you, you are certain that a special understanding exists—that you are, in the end, the one person your friend truly admires and respects. Then some mediocrity walks by,

some vaguely antipathetic character you have never bothered to have a real conversation with, and the friend suddenly turns to him or her. Hey, look who's here! The mediocrity lights up, no longer looking quite so mediocre or antipathetic. Little jokes are told, personal anecdotes exchanged. It is all so plausibly intimate that the person cannot possibly know that he or she actually means nothing to the friend, that you are the person the friend really cares about. Then you look at the mediocrity's face, and suddenly you realize that this is exactly what the mediocrity is thinking about you. It is a glimpse into the abyss. (Menand 1-2)

The passage testifies to the debilitating and disillusioning effects of personal charm as it has its way with others. How are they supposed to feel when witnessing their benefactor's captivating attentions bestowed on someone else? What primarily interests Fitzgerald, though, is the damage to the person *exerting* the charm, the one who feels forever compelled to elicit the love of others, and especially that of women—another parallel between the fictional Diver and the real Clinton.

In the "General Plan" for *Tender Is the Night* that he formulated in 1932, Fitzgerald made it clear that he did not intend to portray Nicole's schizophrenia in clinical terms. "Only suggest from the most remote facts. Not like doctor's stories" or a novelized Krafft-Ebing. "Better Ophelia and her flowers" (MJB, *Composition* 81). In the novel itself, Fitzgerald alludes to Ophelia only once, when Dick, though beaten down and low on energy, is awakened late at night and summoned to rescue Mary North Minghetti and Lady Caroline Sibly-Biers from their cross-dressing misadventure. He doesn't give a damn about the women but feels compelled to use "the old fatal pleasingness, the old forceful charm" on their behalf "because it had early become a habit to be loved." That same compulsion had driven him to make his choice at Dohmler's clinic on the Zürichsee, to choose his Ophelia, to choose the sweet poison (338).

Nicole is not "the rose of Elsinore," to be sure, but instead—one might say—the rose of Lake Forest; she, like Tom Buchanan and Josephine Perry, derived from that exurban enclave of wealth and privilege north of Chicago that the young Princetonian Scott Fitzgerald, son of a failed businessman and knowing he would never have enough coins in his pockets to impress the uncapturable Ginevra King, thought of as the most romantic place on earth.

Nicole comes to the clinic to undergo treatment for schizophrenia, her illness brought on by her father's sexual violation. On the strength of a single brief meeting there in 1917 with Dick Diver, newly in uniform, Nicole initiates a correspondence with her "Capitaine" that has a salutary effect in aiding her recovery. Dr. Diver is circumspect in his letters but does not forget his initial impression of her as "about the prettiest thing" he's ever seen (138).

When the two meet again in April 1919, the seventeen-year-old Nicole still carries the bloom of youth about her, the blossoming quality that Diver cannot resist. Six years later Nicole is still "blooming away and filling the night with graciousness" (47). Nicole and Rosemary in their youth are also compared to horses, Nicole to "a promising colt," Rosemary to "a young mustang" (163, 189). They appeal to Diver because of their budding beauty, but they also are powerful creatures.

Later there will follow "the special girl" in Gstaad; the "flirtatious little brunette," daughter of a patient, whom he kissed "in an idle, almost indulgent way" (an episode that triggers Nicole's near-suicidal relapse); the peasant girl near Savona; the lost girl on the shore of his imaginings; the girl in the garden at Innsbruck; the young English girl at the cabaret in Rome; and, finally, after his dismissal as Nicole's doctor-husband and his exile to upstate New York, the girl who worked at the grocery store in Lockport (199-202, 213, 223, 230-31, 252-54, 352).

So in the end we are reminded of how it was for Diver in the beginning, growing up in Buffalo, the son of a clergyman, attracted to girls and worried about whether to put a nickel or a dime in the collection plate "because of the girl who sat in the pew behind" (222)—the incident illustrating the connection between love and money, which, like that between love and war, undergirds the structure of Fitzgerald's novel. He got to be a psychiatrist, Dick confesses, because there was a girl at St. Hilda's at Oxford who went to the same lectures he did (159).

Associated with flowers and gardens throughout, Nicole is most often compared to the rose. It's an appropriate link, for, as Suzanne West points out in her essay "Nicole's Gardens," while the rose is considered the most beautiful of flowers, its thorns make it dangerous (West 85). And dangerous Nicole becomes, when, "almost complete," she begins to reason gaily as a flower, her ego blooming like a great rich rose as she liberates herself from Diver's supervision—"Other women have had lovers. . . . Why shouldn't I?"—and converts herself into the trimmest of gardens to prepare for her rendezvous with Tommy Barban (310, 323). But that was after a decade of marriage. When first introduced, recovering from the trauma of incest, Nicole is presumably innocent and vulnerable. Yet during their outdoor encounters in the spring of 1919, she boldly conveys a message to Dick Diver: take me, love me, marry me. A woman of the world might have gone about courtship less openly, West observes (West 87). Yet to attract a man who wanted above all to be loved, her strategy could hardly have been improved upon.

Fitzgerald crafts three brilliant scenes of seduction early in Book Two. In each of them, Nicole takes charge and triumphs over Dick's reluctance in a pattern strikingly similar to that of Rosemary in Book One. The first two scenes occur on the grounds of the clinic, and in both of them Nicole initiates the action (SD, "Seduction").

On a lovely spring evening in 1919, Nicole Warren walks out of the central building onto the veranda. There she and Dick Diver see each other for the first time in more than a year, their eyes locking "as though they had become entangled." Nicole proposes a series of arrangements to deepen the entanglement. "Shall we sit out here?" she asks Diver, but another patient, a dumpy señora in a shawl, has followed them outside, and as a matter of courtesy Dick groups three chairs together. Conversation ensues, and as the señora waxes expansive on the weather, Nicole and Dick ignore and talk across her. Nicole reveals that she will be leaving the clinic in June—Franz says she's "[p]erfectly well"—and that she and her sister will then go either "somewhere exciting" or somewhere quiet like Lake Como. "Why don't you come to Como?" she asks Dick, audaciously advancing the intimacy between them. The señora intervenes with "Ah, Como," threatening an extended reminiscence, but just then a trio inside the building starts playing the bravura strains of Franz von Suppé's *Light Cavalry*.

Nicole seizes upon this military music to assume command and remove the unwanted third party from the scene. The señora is, after all, a character invented to illustrate the attraction between Dick and Nicole and Nicole's mastery of the situation. (In somewhat similar fashion, later in the novel, other mental patients are brought into the picture and summarily airbrushed in order to characterize the principal players.) Nicole stands up, smiles for Dick her "moving childish smile that was all the lost youth in the world," and announces that "the music's too loud to talk against—suppose we walk around. Buenas noches, Señora." Good night and goodbye. Two steps down the path, Nicole takes Dick's arm and reveals her plan for their next meeting. She will play some phonograph records from America for him, and she knows of a place where they can meet alone. "I'm not under any restraint at all," she assures him. Dick is dazzled by her beauty and the excitement she generates (154-56).

Music and Romance

Diver is then working hard on his research and writing in Zurich. Perhaps that explains why he was late for their record-playing rendezvous a week later. Perhaps he was of two minds about letting the relationship develop. In any event, Nicole is waiting for him in the garden, and when they settle into the private place she has found, secure behind a low wall facing "miles and miles of rolling night," she plays the records that summon up in Switzerland the immediate American past they have missed—Nicole because of her illness, Dick because of his voluntary expatriation.

Fitzgerald conflates in a single paragraph the lyrics of six different popular songs of the period: "They were so sorry, dear; they went down to meet each other in a taxi, honey; they had preferences in smiles and had met in Hindustan, and shortly afterward they must have quarreled, for nobody knew and nobody seemed to care—yet finally one of them had gone and left the other crying, only to feel blue, to feel sad" (123). John Irwin locates five of the songs referred to in this passage: "I'm Sorry I Made You Cry" (1918), "Darktown Strutters' Ball" (1917), "Smiles" (1917), "Hindustan" (1918), and "After You've Gone" (1918). And Fitzgerald scholar Anthony J. Berret adds yet another song embedded in that paragraph: Irving Berlin's 1919 "Nobody Knows (and Nobody Seems to Care)" (156; Irwin 38-39; Berret). As Malcolm Cowley observed, Fitzgerald's fiction is full of clocks and calendars and also of songs that mark the times, songs Fitzgerald might have written himself had he followed the path he began as a Princeton undergraduate, fashioning lyrics for Triangle Club shows.

Yet another song, one that concludes Nicole and Dick's rendezvous, carries the most significance. This is "A Man Without a Woman," published in 1907. Like "Darktown Strutters' Ball," in latter days it has become a standard to be sung aloud in one watering hole or another, often with a piano player carrying the melody. I learned it in college from the Yale Whiffenpoofs at a table down at Mory's. Nicole learned it as a young girl from the family cook, and she turns off the phonograph to sing it for Dick a cappella. She has orchestrated this concert and decided to finish with this number in order to please him. Yet as she begins to sing, he stands up suddenly as if to break off the proceedings.

"You don't like it?" Nicole asks Dick, and again, plaintively, "You like it?" Of course he likes it. With her impromptu song and the winning smile that follows, this beautiful girl is making him "a profound promise of herself for so little, for the beat of a response, the assurance of a complementary vibration. . . . Minute by minute the sweetness drained down into her out of the willow trees, out of the dark world" (156-57).

Why, then, did Dick Diver summarily rise to his feet when Nicole began to sing? And why should we as readers come to attention as well? Because in the scene immediately preceding this one, Nicole's father—the handsome and terrible Devereux Warren—confesses his incestuous violation to Dr. Dohmler, and Franz Gregorovious has passed on the details of that confession to Diver. According to Warren's account, Nicole was only eleven when her mother died, and he felt sorry for the little girl and let her sleep in his bed. Later, they held hands on trips and ignored other people. People sometimes thought they were lovers. And then, one awful day, they were. Before that happened, Warren remembers, "[s]he used to sing to me." So it's a chilling repeat performance she offers to Dr. Diver (148-49).

The lyrics of "A Man Without a Woman," sometimes called "Silver Dollar," prefigure his future, just as Nicole's singing of them recalls her past. Working from memory and not entirely sensitive to scansion, Fitzgerald cites the first and second of the song's three stanzas. The first uses metaphor to underscore its message. "A man without a woman is like a ship without a sail," a boat without a rudder, a kite without a tail, a wreck upon the sand, yet "if there's one thing worse in this universe, it's a woman, I said a woman, it's a woman without a man."

The second stanza introduces the silver dollar motif:

> Now you can roll a silver dollar 'cross the bar-room floor,
> And it'll roll, because it's round,
> A woman never knows what a good man she's got
> Until she turns him down.

That part of the lyric predicts Dick Diver's rejection by Nicole, a point given greater clarity by Fitzgerald's replacing "Until" with "Till after" she turns him down. The third stanza stresses the fickleness of women:

So listen, my honey, listen to me.
I want you to understand
That as a silver dollar goes from hand to hand,
So a woman goes from man to man,
Yes, a woman goes from man to man.

Fitzgerald's songs do more than revisit a period in American culture. They function as part of his storytelling artistry.

Conquest at Caux

A few weeks later Dick and Nicole meet for lunch in Zurich, away from the clinic. She admits that she is very rich ("I forgive you," he says) and radiates so much beauty that Dick must stare down the gaze of an admiring stranger. "[T]he logic of his life" and career, Diver knows, "tended away from the girl," yet "Nicole brought everything to his feet, gifts of sacrificial ambrosia, of worshipping myrtle" (158).

Dr. Diver is obviously conflicted, as the subsequent conference with Doctors Dohmler and Gregorovious demonstrates. Dohmler thinks the romance has gone far enough. "Miss Nicole" is in love with Diver and in no condition to survive a severe breakup. Dick admits that "the question of marrying her has passed through [his] mind," prompting Franz to vehement objections. "What? And donate half your life to being doctor and nurse and all . . . better never see her again!" The three agree that Diver must be as kind as possible while eliminating himself from Nicole's life (159-62).

Diver goes directly from this meeting to the garden outside, where Nicole, "wearing her hope like a corsage at her belt," is ready to hand herself to him "like a basket of flowers" (179). Once again she has scouted out "a new place," a covered woodshed, where they can go to be alone. In a distressing scene, Nicole advances her candidacy to become his wife, reminding him of "the minor accomplishments"—foreign languages, music, drawing—she could pass on to their children. Desperately, she even considers telling him *how* very rich she is. But Dick addresses her as doctor to patient. Go back to America, he advises her, be a debutante, fall in love, get married, "have a perfectly normal life with a houseful of beautiful descendants" (164-65).

That might have been the end, but Dick cannot shake Nicole out of his system. He sees her once, outside the Palace Hotel in Zurich, riding in a magnificent Rolls-Royce with her sister Baby, but passes by without contact. As a warning to himself, he writes a clinical memorandum about the consequences of another onset of her malady under the stresses she will encounter. He briefly resumes an affair with "the telephone girl" from his military post at Bar-sur-Aube, makes plans for a trip back to the States, reads proof for his book, *A Psychology for Psychiatrists*, and projects yet another work whose monumental title runs to forty-eight words. Finally he sets off on a solo bicycle excursion that carries him south through Berne and Lausanne to the mountains above Montreux. There, quite by happenstance, he is thrown together with Nicole once more, and this time she will not be denied (168-69).

On a funicular ride, Dorothy Perkins roses trail into Dick's compartment, and a sign warns passengers not to pick the flowers. Immediately following the roses, Nicole comes tumbling in, accompanied by the young Conte di Marmora. "Hel*lo*," she says. She looks different—she's had her hair bobbed—and is even more enchanting. In her powder-blue sweater and white tennis skirt, "she was the first morning in May" with every "taint of the clinic" gone. Playful and self-assured, she flirtatiously suggests that Dick carry her down the mountain on the handlebars of his bicycle (170-71).

They are both on the way to Caux, but Dick, still resisting Nicole's attraction and fearing he would be a reminder to her "of a world well left behind," resolves to stay at a different hotel. When the mountain train reaches Caux, though, Nicole is at his side, eager and not at all shy. Wasn't he staying at their hotel? No, he's economizing. Well, wouldn't he come to have dinner? No, but he promises to drop in afterward. Nicole introduces her sister, and Dick wheels away on his bicycle to the less expensive hotel where, as he washes up, he cannot stop thinking of all the "unimportant" people who "did not know how much he was loved" (172-73).

Later that evening at the Warrens' hotel, before the third seduction scene, the orchestra plays "Poor Butterfly" (1916), an extremely popular song during and after World War I—Fitzgerald also mentions it in *This Side of Paradise* and *The Beautiful and Damned*. Based on Puccini's *Madama Butterfly*, it tells the sorrowful story of a Japanese maiden in love with an American sailor and waiting forever for his promised return.

Poor Butterfly
'Neath the blossoms waiting,

Poor Butterfly
For she loved him so.

The song saddens Nicole, who must have seen the parallel to her own romantic yearnings, and she leaves the dining room to take a walk.

In Nicole's absence, Baby Warren tells Dick of her plan to make sure that
Nicole is cared for: take her back to Chicago, acquaint her with the crowd at
the University of Chicago, where their father "controls certain chairs and fel-
lowships," and find a doctor for her to marry. Having delivered this proposal,
Baby dispatches the doctor at hand to search for her sister (176).

Dick finds Nicole on the horseshoe path outside the hotel, where the
lights of Montreux and Vevey and even Lausanne can be seen two thousand
feet below. Nicole probably anticipated that he would come. Certainly she
has a plan in mind. She begins modestly enough.

"You like me?"
"Of course."

Then the crucial questions as they stroll toward the dark end of the horseshoe
walk. If she hadn't been sick, would *he* . . . ? Would *she* have been the sort of
girl . . . ? "He was in for it now," Dick realizes, catching his breath as Nicole
comes near. He tries to make light of the moment, but Nicole rebels. "Bull!"
she interrupts him, and goes on to declare that she knows: knows he's the
most attractive man she's ever met, knows everything about him.

Dr. Diver tries one last time to end matters. "You're a fetching kid," he
says, "but I couldn't fall in love."

"You won't give me a chance," she says, startling him with her imperti-
nence, and, still bolder, moving close. "Give me a chance now."

As they passionately embrace, Dick is carried away. Cannons fire, rain
comes down in sheets, lightning crashes, thunder roars. The Warrens will not
need to buy a doctor for Nicole in "the intellectual stockyards on the South
Side of Chicago." The seduction of Dick Diver is complete.

Fitzgerald takes us inside Nicole's mind as she rejoices in her conquest.
"She felt: There, that'll show him, how conceited; how he could do with me;
oh, wasn't it wonderful! I've got him, he's mine." Nicole has won Dr. Diver.
He is hers, and will continue to be hers as long as he is useful (177-79).

III. BABY WARREN AND DIVER'S DOWNFALL

When Franz Gregorovious ("Dr. Gregory" to his patients) tells Dick Diver about Nicole's progress, he mentions that she is not particularly close to her sister Beth Evan Warren ("Baby" to practically everyone). And, indeed, there are important differences between the two women. Baby is six years older than Nicole, and though afflicted with a terminal case of Anglophilia, not in need of psychiatric care. She regards it as her obligation to oversee the family fortune—the Warrens are famously rich—and to make sure that Nicole's illness has the best possible outcome.

That high-minded goal, though, is accompanied by a hardness of heart that diminishes people into pawns to be maneuvered as necessary. Immediately following Nicole's conquest of Dick at Caux ("he's mine"), Baby asks him to accompany her sister on her return to the sanitarium, effectively ending his bicycle trip. It's not as if Baby particularly wants to throw them together. She thinks Diver too intellectual and too accommodating to qualify as her idea of an aristocrat or ideal husband for Nicole. "She only wanted to use him innocently as a convenience," a telling one-sentence paragraph explains (181).

Baby's casual manipulation of others resembles that of Tom Buchanan in *The Great Gatsby*. Both of them come from Lake Forest, the summer headquarters of Chicago's very rich, where they have learned to reduce human beings of inferior social status into mere commodities. In several scenes in Book Two, a section of the novel that she dominates, Baby converts Dick into a possession, destroying any chance of a successful marriage. The Warrens end up owning Diver. Nicole "led a lonely life, owning Dick who did not want to be owned" (206).

An inescapable tension lurks in every encounter between Dr. Diver and Baby Warren, arising from her apparent ignorance of her father's incestuous behavior. At their first meeting, Baby announces her belief that Nicole had "had some shock" and that she thinks "a boy" was probably responsible. "Father says he would have shot him if he could have found out" (175). Dick knows how wrong she is and how Devereux Warren's encouragement of this mistaken view further damns him, but as a professional he is not in a position to tell Baby about the incest. Perhaps, he reflects, she suspected "the rotted old truth, the real reason for Nicole's illness," but if so she had denied it to herself and swept it back inside a "dusty closet" (244).

Scene 1: The Insult

Over lunch at a restaurant in Zurich, Baby accuses Dick of mercenary motives for attempting to marry into the Warren fortune. She delivers the insult with the authority of "an American ducal family" whose very name caused "a psychological metamorphosis in people." Manifestly, Dr. Diver is Not Her Sort. But even if he isn't an "adventurer," she tells him, who is he anyway? Dick subdues his anger and responds matter-of-factly. He's a doctor, he went to Yale and became a Rhodes Scholar, his father was a clergyman in Buffalo, his great-grandfather governor of North Carolina, and—once more introducing the military motif—he's a direct descendant of Mad Anthony Wayne, one of Washington's Revolutionary War generals. "I think there's enough madness in this affair," the uncomprehending Baby responds, prompting Dick to shake his head hopelessly. Had Nicole not at that stage appeared, "glowing away, white and fresh and new in the September afternoon," Dick might well have flung the marriage in Baby's face (182-83).

The marriage goes ahead when Nicole agrees to the financial terms that Baby and her lawyer impose, and Fitzgerald zooms by the next six years in but four pages, as recorded inside Nicole's consciousness. Two calm years in Zurich, two children ("everything got dark" again after Topsy's birth), a period of travel to Australia and Africa, and then the house above the Mediterranean where they were living when Rosemary Hoyt sunned into the scene. Baby made building that house possible—in the process demonstrating her martial power—by "twitch[ing] wires" in Paris to overcome the objections of French navy officials alarmed upon learning that "Americans had bought part of a hill village" and, the French feared, were liable to turn it into an armed garrison (185).

Scene 2: The Proposition

By the end of 1925, the relationship of Dick and Nicole has reached a "perfect balance," as Bruce L. Grenberg's insightful essay demonstrates. Dick feels diminished by Nicole's rapidly increasing income and begins to neglect his professional life. He goes to his studio regularly, but not much gets done: instead he's "listening to the buzz of the electric clock, listening to time." Meanwhile Nicole, his wife and sole patient, is going through a restorative period of seeming to be well again (Grenberg 122-23).

At this point of stasis they go to the Swiss Alps for Christmas—not St. Moritz, where "the Sturmtruppen of the rich" (127) congregated, but the less fashionable Gstaad. Baby joins them there, feeling that she's made "a gesture of renunciation" in doing so, and she brings along two Englishmen, one young and one old, for her amusement. Dick, sidelined from skiing by a minor injury, distracts himself by conducting a silent flirtation with a "special" one of the "ickle durls" that Nicole, aware of his tendencies, edgily suggests he might dance with in the afternoons.

Then, unexpectedly, Franz shows up with a business proposal. He knows of a clinic on the Zugersee that is coming up for sale and urges Dick to join him as dual owner, Diver as the "brilliant" theoretician, Gregorovious as the operating manager. It would not take up all of Dick's time—he could come and go as was most convenient—but would give him the opportunity to write about the mental illness of actual patients, like such psychiatrists (Franz ticks them off) as Jung, Bleuler, Freud, Forel, Adler. And, he adds, the clinic would offer Nicole a healthy regularity unavailable elsewhere. The only problem is money, and they'd need two hundred and twenty thousand dollars to get started. Dick doesn't have it, or a tenth of it, but Nicole and Baby are "rich as Croesus."

Baby Warren, listening, reflects that she'd feel "quite safe" about her sister living beside a clinic, and she intervenes, advising Dick that *he* ought to consider the proposal and then, going further, saying that *we* must think it over carefully. Diver well understands the implication behind that imperial "we": that the Warrens own him and it's absurd of him to "pretend otherwise." An "emergent Amazon," she is quite unable to grasp how deeply her attack on Dick's pride has wounded him. Offended, he objects that after all it's his decision to make, that he's not at all sure that he likes the idea of being "anchored in Zürich," and that it will take weeks to decide. Only two days later, though, he tells Franz that he's thinking favorably about the idea. Baby, he knows, is "a trivial, selfish woman," but life on the increasingly expensive and fashionable Riviera has been exerting a strain on Nicole, and he is ready to capitulate (197-205).

Scene 3: *The Roman Misadventure*

On shipboard returning from his father's funeral, Diver runs into Albert McKisco, who has enjoyed some success as a novelist since surviving his duel with Tommy Barban and emerging the better for it: less handicapped by an annoying sense of inferiority and becomingly modest about his work. McKisco realizes that his present "vogue" derives more from his vitality than his talent, and in this respect he functions in contrast to Diver, who twice within a few pages is described as suffering from "a lesion of enthusiasm" (236), a lesion of vitality.

Their boat docks in Naples, and Dick has a rendezvous to keep with Rosemary Hoyt in Rome. On the night train between the cities, Diver goes out of his way to brighten the journey for a "lost and miserable" family of two girls and their mother, acting out of an "overwhelming desire to help, or to be admired." Too much wine accompanies this exercise of charm, and he arrives at Rome's Hotel Quirinale early in the morning, exhausted and unshaven. Rosemary is in the lobby, on her way to the day's filming, her beauty groomed like that of "a young horse dosed with black seed oil" (235), and Dick holds himself erect, hoping to conceal his fatigue as Rosemary directs him to phone her that afternoon.

A reversal of roles, paralleling that of McKisco and Diver, has developed during the three years since they last saw each other. Rosemary has grown from an impressionable young girl into a professional woman of the world, and she dominates the diminished Diver, now uncertain about himself and beset by jealousy of the men she must have encountered.

It is understood that they will consummate their affair in Rome, but Rosemary determines where and when. Not during that first afternoon in her hotel room, when she ends passionate kissing with a whispered "No, not now—those things are rhythmic" (239). Not that evening, for she has another commitment. Not until the following afternoon, after Rosemary takes Dick along to the set of *The Grandeur That Was Rome* and exhibits her newly developed sex appeal in scenes with her costar, the leopard-skin-costumed Nicotera. Then, after a lunch fueled by liquor, "[s]he wanted to be taken, and she was" (242).

That single copulation, though, makes neither lover happy. Despite realizing afterward that he was not in love with Rosemary, Dick tortures himself with a series of jealous inquiries about Rosemary's sex life. How many men? Oh, six hundred and forty, she humorously responds (240). Who were they? She will not say. What Dick forces her into saying, however, firmly demolishes any future entanglements. First, she points out that it had been "different" between them in Paris, when she saw Dick at his best, full of enthusiasm and charm, with a young girl's romantic adoration. Second, that Nicotera—whom Dick callously calls "a spic"—has asked her to marry him, prompting a devastating question. She loves Dick, Rosemary insists; there's never been anybody like him. "*But what have you got for me?*" Both of them are in distress when they part. "I guess I'm the Black Death," Dick confesses. He doesn't "bring people happiness any more" (247-48).

Rosemary was the woman Dick had "made the Mediterranean crossing" to see, but Baby Warren's presence in Rome comes as a surprise. Meeting unexpectedly, they engage in a startlingly forthright talk about Nicole's treatment. It's possible, Dick remarks, that he "was the wrong person" for Nicole, prompting Baby to say insensitively that if "somebody else" would make her sister happier, "it could be arranged" (244-45). During the next twenty-four hours she exhibits her ability to arrange difficult matters involving Dr. Diver.

Dick is so thoroughly disillusioned that he turns down Rosemary's offer to forgo a cast party and spend a last evening with him. Instead, he goes nightclubbing with the young Yalie, Collis Clay, flirts with a clearly compliant English girl, drinks himself into a stupor, argues fiercely with taxi drivers over an inflated fare, slugs a policeman, and is badly beaten and thrown into a jail cell. In his distress, Dick bribes one of the taxi drivers to go to the Excelsior Hotel and tell Miss Warren of his plight. It's nearly four a.m. when Baby gets the news and swings into action, using her wealth and social position and determination to secure the reluctant aid of the American consul for her brother-in-law's release.

Fitzgerald generalizes her victory as an example of the power of "the American woman, aroused . . . that had broken the moral back of a race and made a nursery out of a continent." As for Diver, he has suffered a loss of dignity so severe that he will never be the same person again, for "[n]o mature Aryan is able to profit by a humiliation" (263). The beating Dick is subjected to in the Roman police station leaves him with an actual and figurative loss of vision, and it functions like the scene at the Paris train station to mark a crucial turning point in the narrative. When he descends to using Baby's money and influence to buy his way out of jail, he cedes all authority and independence to the Warren clan. Whatever his previous record, Baby reflects afterward, they now possessed a superiority over him for as long as he proved of use. So Book Two ends, leaving the painful litany of Diver's decline and fall yet to be chronicled.

IV. TWO VULNERABILITIES: SEX AND DRINK

Dick Diver comes up with three different excuses to explain his delay in returning to the clinic from Rome and his battered condition when he does. He's had the grippe, he cables Franz. And the scarring around his eyes was caused either by boxing on his transatlantic voyage, as he assures Franz, or by going to the rescue of a drunken friend, the version he tells Nicole.

Kaethe Gregorovious will have none of it. She complains to her husband about Nicole's shying away from her physically, as if she *"smelt* bad" (270). And indeed it is the smell of sweat, and possibly cauliflower, that makes Nicole back away from her. Franz reminds Kaethe to tread warily, for Nicole's money has made their clinic possible. Similarly, he warns his wife not to rush to judgment in her remarks about Dick's appearance: he's "been on a debauch," Kaethe insists, and is no longer "a serious man" (271). Not so, Franz maintains, Dick is most certainly a serious man, and a brilliant one as well, but Kaethe's argument (and the persistent smell of liquor on Diver's breath) eventually persuades Franz that steps must be taken to liberate the clinic from his influence.

As a preliminary step, Franz dispatches Dick to examine a potential patient in Lausanne. "What is it?" Dick asks. "Alcoholism? Homosexuality?" (274). In this case, both. Señor Pardo y Cuidad Real has tried drastic measures to cure his son Francisco of his "corrupt" behavior, including nightly visits to a bordello and lashing the lad with a whip, and he pleads with Diver to take his son back to the clinic for a cure. The doctor interviews the twenty-year-old, a likable lad but in Diver's opinion a nearly hopeless case, both unable to change his sex drive and the drinking that stimulated it.

Sex and liquor also figure prominently in two other chance Lausanne encounters, first with Royal Dumphry, one of the gay men who attended the Divers' party five years earlier, and then with Devereux Warren, expected to die momentarily, alcoholism having done most of the damage. In a meeting with Diver, Warren admits his guilt and pleads for ten minutes with Nicole to send him "happy out of this world" (279). After this confession, Warren unaccountably recovers energy and, having belted down four drinks, leaves Lausanne, presumably to return to Chicago.

This Lausanne incident combines two of the irregular sexual practices that exemplify the contemporary deterioration of society in *Tender Is the Night*. The worst of these, manifestly, is Warren's incestuous invasion of his daughter, with its terrible consequences. This theme is further developed in Rosemary Hoyt's popular film *Daddy's Girl*, with its depiction of a father-daughter complex so sentimentalized as to make Dick, like "all psychologists," wince (81). Diver is certainly not guilty of raping a five-year-old girl, as the booing mob outside the Roman jail mistakenly assumes. Yet from beginning to end, from Nicole and Rosemary to the young girl who worked in a grocery store in Lockport, New York, the novel repeatedly demonstrates his inability to resist the attraction of girls in the first bloom of beauty. And further, during his deterioration, Diver conjures up a series of fleeting and imaginary romances with girls he does not even talk to. "He was in love with every pretty woman he saw now," Fitzgerald tells us, "their forms at a distance, their shadows on a wall" (230).

Gay sexuality is for the most part treated comically. Campion and Dumphry are blatantly effeminate figures, and Dick and Nicole mock their orientation in the beach scene where the doctor changes into what are apparently transparent black lace drawers, but are actually lined with flesh-colored cloth. "Well, if that isn't a pansy's trick," McKisco comments, before apologizing to the two homosexuals (28). Francisco, the Chilean youth, subjected by his father to a month's experience in a Spanish brothel, was known at King's College, Cambridge, as "the Queen of Chile" (275). Yet the youth has a certain dignity.

Lesbianism, however, is scornfully depicted throughout, and in particular at the party in the Rue Monsieur where Dick takes Rosemary one late afternoon in Paris. "You're not going to like these people" (82), he warns her, and indeed she does not. "It was an electric-like shock, . . . perverted as a breakfast of oatmeal and hashish, to cross that threshold" and be confronted by the "neat, slick girl with a lovely boy's face" who tries to secure an assignation with Rosemary and by the tall slender girls, their small heads waving gracefully "rather like long-stemmed flowers and rather like cobras' hoods" (83-84). The "Wanda Breasted" episode cut from Fitzgerald's first draft of the novel and resurrected by Malcolm Cowley as an appendix to his reorganized version of Tender Is the Night condemns the lesbian demimonde still more forcefully. "God damn these women!" (Tender [1951], 345), the protagonist Francis Melarky thinks, after discovering that Wanda, whom he desired, was "a hysterical Lesbian." Scott and Zelda Fitzgerald had experience in such Parisian circles. They'd visited Natalie Barney's lesbian salon at least twice and seen Romaine Brooks's painting of Barney in male attire and wielding a whip. Scott was worried about Zelda's relationship with Oscar Wilde's niece Dolly Wilde, and he felt sure that Zelda had fallen in love with the cool and beautiful Lubov Egorova, her ballet instructor.

These incidents of sexual irregularity stand as evidence of the postwar collapse of the values bequeathed to Dick Diver by previous generations.

They provide context for the series of excruciating events documenting the deterioration of the novel's once-masterful protagonist in the last year of his marriage, as liquor fuels his descent.

We begin with the vociferous complaints of a father whose young son, Von Cohn Morris, is being treated at the clinic. Twice in a month, the lad has smelled liquor on Dr. Diver's breath, and that is two times too many for his fanatically pro-temperance father, who unleashes a rant against "Drink— black drink." In defending himself against Morris's diatribe, Dick objects that people should not be expected to give up "what they regard as food" (285) to please their patients (an echo of Fitzgerald's defense against his wife's doctors' demands that he stop or slow down his drinking, at the very time he was writing *Tender*). This further infuriates Morris, who publicly and angrily withdraws his son from treatment.

The incident has the effect of prompting Diver to reflect on his drinking habits: as he reconstructs them, they include claret with meals, a nightcap, and occasionally an afternoon jolt of gin—altogether an average of half a pint of alcohol a day, "too much for his system to burn up" (286). As a corrective, Diver resolves to cut his daily consumption in half, and with this resolve in mind goes to meet Franz Gregorovious, who has returned from a mountain climbing holiday to discover the trouble at the clinic. "You must know I'm the last man to abuse liquor," Diver begins, but (with Kaethe's encouragement) Franz does not know that at all. Instead, for the second time he proposes a "leave of abstinence" for Dick. "Absence," Diver corrects him, yet Franz's repeated misuse of the word underlies the gravity of the situation.

Suddenly, Diver realizes that their professional relationship has ended. "This is no go," he says (287). Perhaps Franz could pay them back for their investment, Dick suggests, only to find that his partner, one steady Swiss step ahead of him, has already secured such financing. His time at the clinic over, Dick takes Nicole on a long journey around Europe, where with time and money on his hands and only one patient to take care of, he begins to follow the downward path that Abe North traversed before him.

Fitzgerald carefully prepared for this pattern to develop in the final encounters between Abe and Dick in Paris at the end of Book One—most notably, on the occasion of Rosemary's eighteenth birthday, when she more or less simultaneously downs her first glass of champagne and becomes aware of Abe's habit of stopping here and there, wherever, for a drink. What's at stake here is nothing less than Abe's occupation as a composer, his *raison d'être*, that he has given up for drink. In the conversation, Abe lashes out at Dick: "Something tells me I'll have a new score on Broadway long before you've finished your scientific treatise." "I hope so," Dick agreeably responds: he might even "abandon" his treatise (73). This shocks Mary North, and though the following day Dick explains to Rosemary that he is a doctor of medicine and there's no disgrace in not practicing, the fact is that, like Abe before him, he is in the process of losing his profession and his dignity.

As to his professional writing, in his work room at the Villa Diana, Dick pretty much decides to brief his work and publish it in a single undocumented volume. Decision made, he drinks an ounce of gin with twice as much water. Later, it will be two fingers of gin, and a bottle of wine to Nicole's single glass. One can easily skim by such details in the text, but the dramatic effects of the drinking are conveyed in powerful scenes.

V. END AS A MAN

Liberated from his duties at the clinic, Dick begins to spend more time with his children: Lanier, nine, a handsome and inquisitive boy, in a father-son relationship (following the military theme) described as that of "a sympathetic but exacting officer and a respectful enlisted man" (207), and the once-delicate, now-robust daughter Topsy, seven. But even these family duties owe much to the bottle, for it is during "expansive moods over the wines of several countries" (289) that Diver cheerfully talks and plays with his children. With adults, though, liquor arouses a contrarian streak in Dick, so that he repeatedly insults and alienates friends and acquaintances. Nicole objects to this behavior, at first somewhat hesitantly—she is *his* patient, after all—but with developing indignation. Dick Diver drunk is not the man she married, the man who raked the sand and lavished vast quantities of affection on others, the man who loved her enough to devote his life to her recovery.

Scene 1: At the Minghettis
The new version of the Divers, richer than ever, emerges shockingly during their visit to the estate of the Conte di Minghetti and his new wife, Mary North. Nicole has devised an elaborate plan to see that the "great quantity of heavy baggage" that accompanies them arrives safely and securely, marshalling

each item by number. Her system, Fitzgerald reminds us in a military reference, resembled that of "a regimental supply officer who must think of the
bellies and equipment of three thousand men" (290). On the train station
platform, however, the Divers' impressive array of luggage cannot compare
with the Minghettis' welcoming party in this competition between "two
princely households, one of the East, one of the West." Hosain di Minghetti,
whose wealth derived from manganese deposits in Asia, is "not quite light
enough to travel" in a Pullman car south of the Mason-Dixon line. Earlier in
the novel, Mary is a sympathetic figure with a winning smile, bravely trying
to rescue her husband Abe. Now, though, Dick is cynically dubious about
Mary's motives in marrying the wealthy Hosain. If Europe ever goes Bolshe-
vik, he remarks, she'll "turn up as the bride of Stalin" (291).

"Watch your tongue," Nicole warns him, but she is amused, and will-
ingly orders the whiskey Dick requests to alleviate the mountain air, the first
of several drinks that lead to an embarrassing attack on Hosain's gullibility
about all things American over dinner. Specifically, Diver assures his host that
hotel guests in Hollywood were automatically "assigned a harem" and that
a dozen candidates had been sent to his room. This invention, whipped up
by champagne, vividly demonstrates the change in Dick Diver. At his best,
he succeeded in amusing his companions; now he treats them as objects of
ridicule.

Afterward Nicole reproves him. Why so many highballs? Why did he use
the word "spic," as with Nicotera? "Excuse me," Dick sarcastically answers:
he'd meant to say "smoke" (292), compounding the racial intolerance. The
visit turns even uglier with a misunderstanding about whether Lanier had
been bathed in dirty water and Dick's subsequent ordering one of Hosain's
sisters to set things right: a demonstration of *his* failure to understand the
social mores of a different culture. Mary had explained the situation to him,
but he was "too merry" to pay attention. Dr. Diver had once been trained to
listen to others calmly and patiently, but that medically sensible behavior is
no longer operative. At the Minghettis, Fitzgerald shows us Diver bereft of
his charm.

Scenes 2–3: Firing Augustine and Golding's Yacht
When drinking, Dick undergoes a drastic change in personality. And increasingly, with his occupation dwindling away, he drinks almost all the time. The

point is made clear when the Divers' cook Augustine, herself drunk after consuming some of her employers' vintage wines, threatens Dick with a butcher knife and hatchet when he attempts to fire her. She backs up her threats with a series of verbal assaults against Dick, who drinks "all the time" and even, surreptitiously, with workingmen in the town below, and against "disgusting Americans" (298) who come to France to drink up its finest wines. Various threats fail to disarm Augustine, and in the end, humiliated, Dick must resort to bribery to send her on her way. It's reminiscent of the way he uses Baby Warren's money to escape the Roman jail.

At dinner that evening, Nicole confronts her husband about his behavior. He used to want to create things, she says, but now he seems to want "to smash them up" (300). Should they try to go on, or not? What was he getting out of their relationship anyway? "Knowing you're stronger every day," he replies, and then, abruptly changing the subject, proposes that they board T. F. Golding's motor yacht in the harbor. Another bad idea, for on the yacht the Divers encounter two people. One of them will soon be instrumental in ending their marriage, while the other subjects Dick to yet another personal humiliation.

A party is going on as they board the yacht. Nicole discovers Tommy Barban among the guests and, fully aware that he is in love with her, attaches herself to him for the rest of the evening. At dinner Dick is seated next to Lady Caroline Sibly-Biers, currently regarded as "the wickedest woman in London" (303), and launches into the anti-English views that Baby Warren invariably stimulated in him. Lady Caroline more than holds her own in the ensuing exchange of insults, ending with a declaration that Dick had been seen "associating with a questionable crowd in Lausanne": presumably Dumphry and the hapless Chilean youth. "So I am actually a notorious—" (305), Dick responds, with the expansive Golding crushing out the phrase.

After this incident, Diver—quite drunk—becomes passive and withdrawn. Nicole is less than supportive, feeling furious about her husband's "having become fuddled . . . having come off humiliated" by Lady Caroline's "preposterous statement" (305). When the boat docks in Cannes, Tommy Barban insists on driving them to the Villa Diana and staying overnight. "There are those who can drink and those who can't," he says to Nicole, and "[o]bviously Dick can't." She ought to tell him as much (307). Nicole has not quite reached that level of assertiveness with Dick, but the next morning, she displays the drift of her feelings with a telling gesture. Tommy, beset by a chest cold, is about to leave, and as he prepares to drive away she tosses him the family's only jar of camphor rub (312). Dick objects—there are four of them who may need the medicine—but the choice has been made. A few weeks later, Nicole initiates her affair. During the interim, Dick undergoes yet another in the succession of mortifying failures that make Book Three of *Tender Is the Night* distressing to read for anyone who has developed a sense of identification or sympathy with Fitzgerald's protagonist.

Scenes 4–5: Showing Off for Rosemary and Tommy's Demand

At Yale, Dick Diver had been a gymnast, performing on the rings, and when Rosemary Hoyt unexpectedly swims back into his orbit on an abbreviated visit to Gausse's beach, he attempts, and fails, to perform an acrobatic show of strength for her benefit. Gausse's is not what it was five years before. It's overcrowded, for one thing, and the newly rich Mary Minghetti rules as its queen. On the morning of Rosemary's appearance there, Dick follows the actress to a motorboat, where she joins a youngish group of admirers about to try their skill on the aquaplane. Diver has a special talent for the board; on the Zugersee the previous summer, he had hoisted a 200-pound man onto his shoulders and stood up. To impress Rosemary, he attempts to perform this stunt again. It should be easier, for the volunteer youths he tries to lift weigh only around 150 pounds. But the Divers' pattern of living and indulgence in drink have taken a physical as well as a psychological toll. He tries and fails, four times in all, ending so exhausted that he himself must be dragged onto the motorboat.

It is a pitiful display, and to alleviate the embarrassment Dick comments that he couldn't have "lifted a paper doll" (319) on his last attempt. Nicole is not amused. She had been close to panic as she watched her husband fail one time after another and barely escape being struck by the board. In the end, though, her panic turned to contempt: "[E]verything he did annoyed her now." Rosemary doesn't know what to think. She had heard the gossip that Baby Warren's sister had "thrown herself away on a dissipated doctor" who was not "received" anywhere (321). But she wants to think well of him, and he manages to resurrect enough of his former charm to win her over. There follows a rather implausible conversation in which Diver, playing the role of film director, instructs Rosemary how to maintain the full attention of her audience. This inspires Rosemary to ask Topsy if she would like to be an actress when she grows up. However well meant, this question infuriates Nicole, and using the domineering voice of her grandfather, the robber baron who accumulated the family fortune, she dresses Rosemary down for putting such ideas in the heads of other people's children.

This show of strength on Nicole's part is soon joined by a rare demonstration of everyday dominance. She'll drive the car home, she tells Dick—something she hadn't done for months—and en route she acquires a tremendous burst of independence and self-confidence. She hated the beach, where for so long she had played planet to Dick's sun. She is ready to live another, very different life, so she writes "a short provocative letter" (323) to Tommy Barban, knowing that it will bring an end to her marriage. Dick, arriving home later, seems to sense what's on Nicole's mind and drives off to Provence to facilitate his wife's rendezvous with Tommy.

Their affair is consummated at a shore hotel in Nice, where their love-making is followed by a naval quarrel (a fight between two sailors from the American battleship on the water), by the "Cr-ACK—BOOM-M-m-m" (331) of the ship sounding recall, and by an invasion of their room by the *poules* who want to wave from the balcony at their sailors as they board ship, all providing a military background and cheapening Nicole and Tommy's sexual bond with the introduction of the ship-following whores.

Dick does not put up a struggle when, shortly thereafter, Tommy—who is now Nicole's lover—demands a confrontation. The scene parallels the Plaza Hotel battle for Daisy between Jay Gatsby and Tom Buchanan in *The Great Gatsby*, but all the drama is missing in the later novel. Dick quietly yields to Tommy's declaration that Nicole loves him, not her husband.

This showdown occurs on a day when Dick and Nicole jointly venture to the barber-beauty shop, she to have her hair cut, he for a shave. Tommy Barban, driving by, spies them there and rushes into the shop to deliver his ultimatum. "He wants to see us together," Dick tells Nicole, "so I agreed to have it over with" (343). Almost comically, the Divers—her hair half cut, his shave half done—go off to a cafe where Tommy can make his case. To get through the ordeal, Dick first orders a scotch, then changes it to *two* gins. Nicole tries to soften the blow. Wouldn't Dick be happier without her to care for, she asks? Wouldn't he have more time for his work as a writer on psychiatry? By contrast, militant as ever, Tommy threatens Dick with dire consequences should he make any physical overtures toward Nicole, but Tommy misunderstands the situation. Since the camphor rub incident, Dick has understood what will and must happen. He knows that his medical and conjugal services to Nicole are no longer required, and he will not offer any opposition.

Oddly, at just this time crowds assemble outside the cafe to watch the riders in the Tour de France pedal past, establishing an echo for Baby Warren's scathing dismissal of Dick. He was socially unsuited and beyond his depth in his role as Nicole's husband, she concludes. "We should have let him confine himself to his bicycle excursions" (349).

Fitzgerald did not want to end his novel on this defeatist theme, with the almost overwhelmingly poignant series of Diver's failures. As a counter measure, he created two scenes where his protagonist is shown exercising his charm and energy on behalf of two women he neither likes nor respects: Lady Caroline Sibly-Biers and Mary Minghetti.

Inasmuch as it was Lady Caroline who announced the rumor of Dick's homosexuality on Golding's yacht, there is an obvious irony of situation in Dick's rescue of the two from the authorities after they are caught for cross-dressing in French sailors' uniforms, picking up two young girls, and taking them to a "lodging-house," presumably for sexual satisfaction. This, apparently, is characteristic of Lady Caroline's behavior as the wickedest woman in London, or in this case on the Riviera, where she and Mary Minghetti are apprehended for their offenses and brought to the Antibes police station. Diver manages to persuade the chief to drop all charges against the two by exaggerating their social standing—Mary is the niece of "Lord Henry Ford" and Caroline "affianced to the brother of the Prince of Wales" (341)—and by distributing bribes to the chief, the two girls, the outraged father of one of them, and just about everyone involved. In this basically comic scene (Gausse, serving as Dick's attendant, kicks the entirely unapologetic Lady Caroline in the backside), Dick acquires a measure of the dignity and responsibility he'd exhibited early in the novel.

In the serial version of the novel, Perkins asked Fitzgerald to cut this scene from 1250 to 800 words, but the author balked at this editorial directive, actually *adding* 150 words. Otherwise, he pointed out, Dick's "character" weakens. The scene itself was written to "bolster" him in his "undignified cuckold situation" (SD, "History" 194-95).

Similarly, Diver is given yet another opportunity, in the final pages, to exhibit a semblance of the charm so vividly on display in Book One. It is his last day on the Riviera, and Dick continues his habitual drinking, taking a healthy slug of brandy before saying goodbye to the children and then downing anisette on Gausse's terrace with Mary Minghetti, so that by late morning he is "already well in advance of the day." In revision Fitzgerald made significant deletions from two drafts of this scene, both of which ended with Dr. Diver intoxicated: in one case falling on his face and in the other helped away by a waiter. In the finished novel, after managing with calculated insincerity to renew Mary's admiration for him, Dick sways a little when he stands up to bless the beach below. He does not require assistance. In his one-page dying-fall summary, Fitzgerald sends Diver off to exile somewhere in the Finger Lakes district of upstate New York. It would have been too great an indignity, Fitzgerald must have decided, to have him exit staggering.

It's not that Diver behaves particularly admirably in his dealings with the provincial police chief—money, more than guile, earns the women's release—or in his final manipulation of Mary Minghetti, when to win her affection he pretends that "there has always been something" (351) between them. The book begins and ends with Diver putting on a show for others, innocently raking the sand on Gausse's beach in the first scene, looking down at the beach as he has his easy way with Mary in the last. He may feel a private revulsion while keeping the two women from incarceration and practicing his old social skills to charm Mary. But he does manage to succeed in these episodes, alleviating a long string of failures. It was "legitimate to ruin Dick," as Fitzgerald explained the ending to Perkins, "but . . . by no means legitimate to make him ineffectual" (SD, "History" 194).

VI. CASUALTIES: DICOLE

The Vampire Motif

As biographer Henry Dan Piper concluded, Fitzgerald "really did not know enough about psychiatry to treat it authoritatively" (Piper 222-23). He learned much from Zelda's doctors and from his psychiatrist friend (and possibly lover) Margaret Egloff, but manifestly did not fully understand the concept of transference in the psychoanalytic process, converting a complex interaction between patient and doctor into a simple transfer of energy. So in his 1932 "General Plan" for the novel, Nicole's "transference" to Dick "saves her" sanity—transference, that is, in the sense of a draining of vitality from her doctor to herself (MJB, *Composition* 80).

As we shall see, this interpretation clearly derived from Fitzgerald's conflict in his own marriage. And it nicely fit his conviction that men and women were waging a combat for survival, with the women winning. On that basis, as a 1935 review in the *Journal of Mental and Nervous Disease* observed, the novel was "of special value" to psychiatrists and psychoanalysts "as a probing study of some of the major dynamic interlockings in marriage" (SD, "History" 187).

The best study of this issue, James W. Tuttleton's "Vitality and Vampirism in *Tender Is the Night*," traces the prevalence of vampirism throughout Fitzgerald's writing, particularly as borrowed from John Keats's "La Belle Dame sans Merci." In that poem, a knight encounters a beautiful lady who lures him to her "elfin grot" for lovemaking and afterward lulls him to sleep. He dreams of pale warriors who cry out to him that "La belle dame sans merci / Hath thee in thrall" and awakens weak and bloodless, the beautiful faery child having enchanted him into a living death.

Fitzgerald was particularly fond of that poem. He wrote its theme of a woman using her supernatural powers to conquer and subdue a male adversary into all of his major work. He cites it in *This Side of Paradise* and at one time planned to name his second novel *The Beautiful Lady without Mercy* rather than *The Beautiful and Damned*. His lifelong admiration for Keats is further reflected in selecting the title *Tender Is the Night* title from the passage in "Ode to a Nightingale" that serves as an epigraph for the novel.

> *Already with thee! tender is the night . . .*
> *. . . But here there is no light,*
> *Save what from heaven is with the breezes blown*
> *Through verdurous glooms and winding mossy ways.*

Tender Is the Night itself is rife with references to Dick's loss of vitality, his lesion of energy and enthusiasm, as contrasted both with Rosemary's professional vitality and, more importantly, with Nicole's remarkable surge in health in an apparent exchange for her husband-doctor's loss. In this fashion, as Tuttleton observes, Fitzgerald transposes the theme of vampirism into a psychiatric transference or counter-transference between his two major characters (Tuttleton 238-42).

Relapses and Recovery

Franz had warned Dick that in nineteen cases out of twenty, the initial achievement of mental health would later result in relapses, and so it happens with Nicole. At first both marriage partners thought of themselves as closely aligned with each other: hence Dick's practice of signing letters as "Dicole" and Nicole's mentioning that when she chats with Mary it is as if Dick were talking. But of course they are not at all the same person. Fitzgerald underlines the differences in a series of internal monologues early in Book Two that take us inside Nicole's thoughts and substitute for scenes as a way of carrying the narrative forward. One such use of her consciousness begins with a reminiscence of Nicole's premarital meeting with the family attorney ("How do you do, lawyer" [183]) and agreeing to financial arrangements Baby has stipulated for her, so that Nicole will have authority to spend rather less than half of the inheritance she is supposed to share equally with her sister. Nicole's introspective reflections go on to telescope the subsequent years— her dark periods (the worst after Topsy's birth) and the travel Dick arranged to brighten the days.

The most severe of Nicole's relapses is triggered by Dick's careless kissing of a young girl, the daughter of one of his mental patients at the Zugersee clinic. As a consequence, the patient, the girl's mother, writes Nicole an incendiary letter accusing Dick "in no uncertain terms of having seduced her daughter." This charge is false: Dick stopped the flirtation after the one "almost indulgent" kiss (213). But Nicole, keenly aware of her husband's attraction to blooming teenagers, is driven by jealous anger into near-homicidal mania.

This crisis occurs after the Diver family visits the Agiri fair, where Nicole is unable to "fix her attention" except on a Punch and Judy show, a performance that ends in comic violence when the puppet Punch violently attacks his Judy. Nicole then runs away from her husband and children, and on being relocated, pleads with Dick to help her in her extremity. But he has no ready solution for her madness, and worse, "could not watch her disintegrations without participating in them." On the mountainous drive home, Nicole wrests the steering wheel from Dick's control, very nearly plunging all four passengers to their deaths. Afterward she laughs manically and exults in her demonstration of power. "You were scared, weren't you?" she tells Dick. "You wanted to live!" (214-20).

In this frightening passage, Nicole emerges as a powerful force capable of destroying her husband and children. Thereafter, with her descent into madness behind her yet no longer subservient to the direction of her husband-doctor, Nicole manages to increase the hardness, inherited from her family, that Rosemary detected in her at the beginning of the novel. As she weathers her relapses, she toughens into Georgia pine. Similarly, her eyes, "green" and "grey" in Books One and Two, are transformed into "white crook's eyes" near the end, eyes resembling those of the disreputable Sid Warren, her horse-trading grandfather and source of the family fortune. These eyes turn "whitest" of all as she watches Dick, truly at liberty, walk away downcast from the final confrontation with Tommy. Nicole also speaks in "her grandfather's voice" when she castigates Rosemary for asking Topsy whether she might want to be an actress. Blood tells—"better a sane crook than a mad puritan," she decides (328)—and so does the authority it conveys.

She has always had the capacity to exert control over others. Her design of the rooms for the most psychologically dangerous patients at the Zugersee clinic, for example, conceals "strong, unyielding" (209) restraints beneath a veneer of seemingly delicate filigree work. And when Mary Minghetti confronts her with the accusation that Lanier may have lied about bathing in dirty water, she throws on her clothes "as though they were chain mail" (295). This innate quality gives Nicole an advantage in the struggle for dominance with Dick in Book Three, a struggle repeatedly couched in martial terms.

Nicole at the end, now almost thirty, is contrasted with herself ten years earlier. Fitzgerald describes the American woman of nineteen, an age of insolence, as a "young cadet," and the twenty-nine-year-old one as "a fighter strutting after combat" (325). Thus armored, Nicole becomes equipped to prevail in the marital battle with Dick, finally able to break free from her long subservience to his guidance and care. In their last devastating talk together, the "ruined" Dick admits he can no longer "do anything" for her and must now try to save himself. She lashes back that he's "a coward" who's made a failure of his life and wants to blame it on her. It's a cruel remark, and difficult for her to utter.

> [S]he struggled with it, fighting him with her small, fine eyes, with the plush arrogance of a top dog, with her nascent transference to another man, with the accumulated resentment of years; she fought him with her money and her faith that her sister disliked him, and was behind her now; with the thought of the new enemies he was making with his bitterness; with her quick guile against his wining and dining slowness; her health and beauty against his physical deterioration, her unscrupulousness against his moralities—for this inner battle she used even her weaknesses— . . . And suddenly, in the space of two minutes she

achieved her victory and justified herself to herself without lie or sub-
terfuge, cut the cord forever. (336-37)

"The war is over," so Milton Stern summed matters up; "the new world has
won, and Dr. Richard Diver, American, is dead. Shot through the identification card. No Lazarus, he" (Stern, *Broken* 82).

The Power of the Purse

The Warren money is the greatest asset in Nicole's armory. As Tommy Barban
puts it, Nicole has "too much money ... Dick can't beat that" (327). No, but
he tries to do so, especially during the first years of their decade together. He
pays for his own clothes and personal expenses, travels third-class when alone,
allows himself no extravagances, and maintains "a qualified financial independence" (195). But it isn't easy. His wife has all the money in the world, so
why should they forbid themselves pleasures and conveniences? *Why shouldn't
they* buy up and tear down nine peasant dwellings to make way for their Villa
Diana above the Mediterranean? Over time and "in multiplying ways" Dick's
resistance is worn down "by a trickling of goods and money" (195). He's swal-
lowed up "like a gigolo" (229).

Perhaps most damningly, Diver himself learns to buy his way out of trouble. On the basis of past purchases, he prevails upon the Paris hotelkeeper
McBeth to remove the murdered Jules Peterson from any connection to himself and Nicole or to Rosemary, absolving them of any police involvement
or damaging publicity. He pays an offending taxi driver to summon Baby
Warren to his rescue from a Roman jail cell. He produces one hundred francs
to convince Augustine to put down her carving knife and hatchet. He bribes
the judge in Antibes to liberate Lady Caroline Sibly-Biers and Mary North
Minghetti from prosecution. For the most part, though, these are judicious
actions performed as much for the benefit of others as for himself.

It is not true, as Baby Warren obviously believes and Kaethe Gregorovious actually says, that Dick married Nicole for her money (270), but it is,
of course, her wealth that enables him to achieve these escapes from adver-
sity. This diminishes him, and eventually he dwindles into little more than
his wife's possession. That suits Nicole, who wanted to own him and wanted
him to stand still forever. It's an untenable situation, fated to end badly.

The novel's most impressive display of Nicole's financial power comes in her shopping expedition with Rosemary in Book One. Rosemary shops carefully for what she needs—dresses for herself, gifts for friends and professionals—with money she has earned. Nicole shops with no thought of the cost, buying many things and buying them in bulk. Fitzgerald presents the scene with anticapitalist commentary.

> Nicole bought from a list that ran two pages long, and she bought the things in the windows besides. . . . She bought colored beads, folding beach cushions, artificial flowers, honey, a guest bed, bags, scarfs, love birds, miniatures for a doll's house and three yards of some new cloth the color of prawns. She bought a dozen bathing suits, a rubber alligator, a travelling chess set of gold and ivory, big linen handkerchiefs for Abe, two chamois leather jackets of kingfisher blue and burning bush from Hermès. . . . Nicole was the product of much ingenuity and toil. For her sake trains began their run at Chicago and traversed the round belly of the continent to California; chicle factories fumed and link belts grew link by link . . . men mixed toothpaste in vats and drew mouthwash out of copper hogsheads; girls canned tomatoes quickly in August or worked rudely at the Five-and-Tens on Christmas Eve; half-breed Indians toiled on Brazilian coffee plantations and dreamers were muscled out of patent rights in new tractors—these were some of the people who gave a tithe to Nicole, and as the whole system swayed and thundered onward it lent a feverish bloom to such processes of hers as wholesale buying, like the flush of a fireman's face holding his post before a spreading blaze. (65-66)

Rosemary is impressed by the casual grace with which Nicole buys out the store and on another, briefer shopping expedition the two women undertake. "It was fun spending money in the sunlight of the foreign city . . . with the confidence of women lovely to men" (112), she reflects. And if the incipient Marxist in Fitzgerald—in his 1932 General Plan he has the "communist-liberal-idealist" Diver send "his neglected son into Soviet Russia to educate him" (MJB, *Composition* 77)—suggests that Nicole, the "haute bourgeoisie" heiress, contains her fiery doom within herself, his novel makes it clear that others will meet their doom before she does.

Fitzgerald was convinced that something was terribly wrong at the very heart of Western civilization. This conclusion derived from the "dominant supercessive idea" in Oswald Spengler's *Decline of the West*, a book that deeply impressed him. As he wrote Maxwell Perkins in 1927, "Spengler and Marx are the only modern philosophers that still manage to make sense in this horrible mess." Spengler argued that the West was in the throes of a fatal malady. In its final deterioration money would replace aristocracy, and "monied thugs" and "new Caesars" (SD, "History" 185) would take control. It is fitting that our final glimpse of Dick Diver in *Tender Is the Night* should show him courting the now fabulously wealthy Mary Minghetti. It is the summer of 1930, several months after the market crashed on Black Thursday, but as David Brown points out in *Paradise Lost*, she and the other rich on Gausse's beach show no sign of being "seriously questioned, challenged, or even inconvenienced" by the Great Depression ahead. They are "a breed apart ... above it all" (Brown 261).

Book Three of *Tender Is the Night* traces the serial humiliations of Dick Diver as he loses his charm, his energy, his physical strength and agility, his vision, his control, his tolerance, and his dignity. It is painful to read, one of the saddest stories ever written, similar to and yet more moving than the account Fitzgerald would write a year later of his own crack-up. As we—except those hardest of heart—feel sympathy for Diver, we should think as well of the statement Fitzgerald is making in this novel, as in *The Great Gatsby*, about a culture in which the very rich are empowered to buy and discard other people at will.

VII. TO THE LIFE

Early 1930s: The Fitzgeralds in Conflict

~

There is an assumption among literary critics that to provide an account of what was going on in a writer's life at the time [s]he was writing a work of fiction tends to diminish the value of her or his accomplishment. Better to deal directly with the art and ignore the life. But this attitude flies in the face of reality. If Scott Fitzgerald came to think of himself and Zelda as fiercely competitive enemies when he was at long last finishing *Tender Is the Night*, to know about that conflict serves to illuminate our understanding of the novel. The book traces the progress of Nicole Warren Diver from a psychologically damaged teenager to a dominant young woman, and the parallel disintegration of her doctor-husband into a shadow of his once charming and powerful self. This was not what happened to the Fitzgeralds, but it did reflect what Scott feared might happen in what he regarded, ca. 1932–34, as a struggle for survival between himself and his wife. Fitzgerald was not writing directly *about* his own experience in the novel. But he was writing *out of* that experience, a distinction I owe to the poet-professor Donald Junkins.

In *A Moveable Feast,* his memoir that crosses the boundaries between fiction and fact, Ernest Hemingway is hard on Scott Fitzgerald and even harder on Zelda. In the first of three chapters devoted to the Fitzgeralds, Hemingway writes about his first meeting with the three-years-older writer at the Bar Dingo in Montparnasse in the spring of 1925. He describes Scott in manifestly effeminate terms.

> Scott was a man then who looked like a boy with a face between handsome and pretty. He had very fair wavy hair, a high forehead, excited and friendly eyes and a delicate long-lipped Irish mouth that, on a girl, would have been the mouth of a beauty. His chin was well built and he had good ears and a handsome, almost beautiful, unmarked nose. This should not have added up to a pretty face, but that came from the coloring, the very fair hair and the mouth. The mouth worried you until you knew him and then it worried you more. (EH, *Feast* 149)

Despite this unfortunate initial impression, Hemingway had much to learn from Fitzgerald about "the gossip and economics of being a successful writer," and Scott was "very jolly and charming and endearing" in dispensing that knowledge, "even if [here again Hemingway strikes a cautionary note] you were careful about anyone becoming endearing" (EH, *Feast* 153). Then Ernest read *The Great Gatsby,* just published, and on the basis of that superlative novel forgave Scott for his drinking and hypochondria and foolishness and enlisted him as one of his friends. For the next year and a half, theirs was an extremely close friendship.

Very early on, though, Hemingway became aware of the barriers Zelda erected against Scott's success. She is first characterized in *A Moveable Feast* as an adversary who encouraged Scott's alcoholic tendencies because they kept her entertained and rendered him unable to write. Even worse, according to Hemingway, Zelda set about unmanning Scott by maintaining that he had never satisfied her sexually and that he could never make any woman happy because of the way he was built. Hemingway tried to reassure Fitzgerald on this issue by taking him to the men's room for inspection of his equipment and a discourse on the visual effects of foreshortening—or so he wrote in "A Matter of Measurements," his final chapter on the Fitzgeralds. Ernest and Zelda never got along. No one, she thought, could be "as male as all that." And eventually, shortly before her breakdown at the end of 1929, she believed that her husband and Ernest were lovers and said so. The accusation outraged Scott. "The nearest I ever came to leaving you," he wrote her, "was when you told me you thought I was a fairy in the rue Palatine" (SD, *Hemingway vs. Fitzgerald* 159). But no, I do not think that their friendship, which did mean more to Scott than to Ernest, led to their becoming lovers.

Above all, *Tender Is the Night* makes a deeply personal statement about the failure of a marriage beset by Scott's alcoholism, Zelda's mental illness, and the developing dominance of the female in the war between the sexes that D. H. Lawrence foresaw. That message resonated as matters reached a crisis stage during the literary competition between Scott and Zelda.

In good part Scott was at fault for letting such a rivalry develop. He borrowed story ideas from Zelda, and he raided her letters and diaries for use in his own fiction. As she wrote, tongue in cheek, of *The Beautiful and Damned* in 1922, "Mr. Fitzgerald—I believe that is how he spells his name—seems to believe that plagiarism begins at home." These appropriations were relatively innocent, professionally. They became less so when he attempted to capitalize on her writing financially.

On at least two occasions, for example, he sold her stories as his own work, thereby raising their price to the high-paying slick magazines. She wrote the first story, "Our Own Movie Queen," in 1923, or at least most of it, with Scott doing some revisions and altering its climax. It appeared in 1925 under his name, hiking its price to $900. In 1929 and 1930, five of Zelda's short "girl" stories for *College Humor*, about women "who have gotten less from life—and from men and love—than they anticipated," came out as the joint work of "F. Scott and Zelda Fitzgerald," although the diction and narrative approach were manifestly hers alone. Under this false authorship, agent Harold Ober was able to fetch $500 to $800 apiece for these stories. Ober went further in the case of Zelda's "A Millionaire's Girl" (1930), which he judged as worth considerably more than her *College Humor* sketches and sold to the *Saturday Evening Post* as by F. Scott Fitzgerald, commanding his highest payment of $4,000 (FSF and ZF, *Bits* 10-11).

Scott thought enough of Zelda's stories to propose to Max Perkins that they be collected in a book. His tolerance for her work, however, was challenged in March 1932 when Zelda, in a burst of energy while confined to the Phipps Clinic in Baltimore, wrote a draft of a novel called *Save Me the Waltz* and sent it to Perkins for consideration without so much as telling Scott. There was plenty for Scott to object to about that, beginning with his resentment about her ability to produce a book in a short period of time while he was still two years away from finishing *Tender Is the Night*.

In retaliation, Fitzgerald asserted his authority by taking control of Zelda's novel in progress. *Save Me the Waltz* is a highly autobiographical work, recounting in detail how Alabama Beggs, the female protagonist based on Zelda, suffers from her husband's cruelty and infidelities during their time as expatriates in France. Initially she called him Amory Blaine, appropriating the name of Scott's protagonist in *This Side of Paradise*. That would have to change, Scott demanded, and Zelda duly changed Alabama's philandering husband's name to David Knight. In his role as editor-adviser, Scott also mandated a number of other changes as he guided her book through revisions and negotiated about it directly with Perkins. By mid-May he was able to send the amended manuscript to Max with his judgment that it was "a good novel now, perhaps a very good novel—I am too close to it to tell" (SD, *Fool* 81-83). Scribner decided to publish it, with Scott's stipulation that half of any royalties it earned up to $10,000 would be applied to the debt he had run up with his publisher for advances. That provision hardly mattered, for *Save Me the Waltz*, which came out in October 1932, did not sell well and the reviews were indifferent.

Zelda was not discouraged, however. She began to write another work of fiction based on her experience as a psychiatric patient, thereby invading the very territory Scott was exploring in *Tender Is the Night*. This led to the bitter confrontation between husband and wife on 28 May 1933, recorded in a 114-page typescript by a stenographer in the Baltimore office of Dr. Thomas

A. C. Rennie, a colleague of Zelda's doctor Adolf Meyer at Sheppard-Pratt Hospital.

The Confrontation

So there they were, sitting across from each other in the doctor's office, Scott and Zelda: a great writer who because of drink and dissipation was struggling to finish a novel he'd promised to deliver to his publisher time and again, and an amateur talented in several arts fighting against mental illness as she tried to make her own mark as a writer. Zelda's doctors presumably felt that bringing husband and wife together in this way would enable them to resolve their differences. That would not be easy (MJB, *Grandeur* 349-55).

Zelda wanted to continue her career as a writer. Scott adamantly proclaimed that she should not. "Possibly she would have been a genius had we never met," he wrote Dr. Meyer a few weeks earlier. But as matters stood, she was poaching on his material—that is to say, on the events and incidents that troubled them as a married couple. As the professional writer in the family, he believed that material was exclusively his to use. Zelda disagreed, strongly.

There is no question that both relied on their mutual experiences for their fiction. The parallels between *Save Me the Waltz* and *Tender Is the Night* are striking. Alabama Knight has to abandon her engagement as a ballet dancer in Naples to return to the States for her father's funeral. Dick Diver must leave his clinic to cross the Atlantic for his father's funeral. The Knights' daughter Bonnie is given a bath in dirty water, like the one the Divers' son Lanier has at the Minghettis'. David Knight suffers from the same compulsion to please others that undermines Dick Diver, and they both describe it in precisely the same language: "so easy to be loved—so hard to love." Dickie Acton in *Waltz* shoots her lover at the Gare de l'Est, while Maria Wallis in *Tender* shoots hers in the Gare St. Lazare.

"When it came to drawing upon their experiences," Scottie Fitzgerald observed forty years later, "a serious conflict of interest arose between the characters in *Tender Is the Night* and those in my mother's novel, *Save Me the Waltz*" (FSF and ZF, *Bits* 7). And Zelda's book was published first, a year and a half in advance of Scott's.

This conflict lay between them as they began their afternoon talk in Dr. Rennie's office. Determined to prevail in his attempt to stop her writing, Scott wrote himself a memo in advance. "Prepare physically," he wrote, and went on with seven other points of debater's notes. Above all, he reminded himself in caps, "KEEP COOL BUT FIRM" (SD, *Fool* 86). Yet when they faced each other he went on the attack.

"You are a third-rate writer and a third-rate ballet dancer," he told Zelda, while he was "a professional writer with a huge following . . . the highest paid short story writer in the world."

"It seems to me," she retaliated, "that you are making a rather violent attack on a third-rate talent, then." Why should he care what she wrote about? (MJB, *Grandeur* 349).

Because, he insisted, she was "broaching at all times" on his material, picking up crumbs he dropped at the dinner table and putting them into books. She should certainly not have been "sneakingly writing" a novel about insanity, which was both bad for her (as Dr. Rennie believed) and for him, inasmuch as he was also writing about that subject.

At this stage Zelda struck back where she knew he was vulnerable, attributing Scott's bitterness to his extended procrastination over finishing *Tender*. If he ever stopped drinking long enough to get it written, he wouldn't feel "so miserable and suspicious and mean towards everybody else." He'd only stooped to accusing her because he was so "full of self-reproach" (MJB, *Grandeur* 352).

The dialogue turned even worse after these volleys. Both Fitzgeralds insisted that they could not stand living together without a change in their relationship. The previous fall, when Scott came back from New York drunk, Zelda recalled, "you sat down and cried and cried . . . said I had ruined your life and you did not love me and you were sick of me and wished you could get away." She'd prefer an insane asylum to such conditions, she said. Scott volunteered the information that they'd had no sex for three or four months, though prior to that their relations had been very pleasant. "Well," Zelda responded sarcastically, "I am glad you considered them satisfactory" (MJB, *Grandeur* 351).

In the end Scott carried the day, as Zelda with great reluctance accepted his demand that she not write a novel or play about psychiatry, laid on the Riviera or in Switzerland, and furthermore she'd have to submit any ideas for fiction to him for approval. All right, she said to this short-term agreement, but once he'd finished his novel she thought they'd better get a divorce, because she could not live on such terms.

This apparent resolution of their dispute left both Fitzgeralds unsatisfied. Taking his cue from Zelda's final remarks, Scott consulted Baltimore lawyer Edgar Allan Poe (a direct descendant of the famous writer) about a divorce and about the possibility of getting custody of daughter Scottie. In a memorandum among his papers at Princeton's Firestone Library, he spelled out his reasons.

> As I got feeling worse Zelda got mentally better, but it seemed to me that as she did she was also coming to the conclusion she had it on me, if I broke down it justified her whole life—not a very healthy thought to live with about your own wife. . . . Finally four days ago told her frankly & furiously that had got & was getting rotten deal trading my health for her sanity and from now on was going to look out for myself & Scotty exclusively, and let her go to Bedlam for all I cared.

Then, in a more explicit note he outlined a diabolical plan to drive her round the bend.

> *Plan — To attack on all grounds*
> Play (suppress), novel (delay), pictures [he had advocated that she switch her artistic endeavors to painting] (suppress), character (showers??), child (detach), schedule (disorient to cause trouble), no typing
> Probably result—a new breakdown
> Danger to Scotty (?)
> "   " herself (?)
> *All this in secret* (SD, *Fool* 85-86)

There is no evidence that Fitzgerald carried out this scheme, but the mere fact that he was capable of setting it down on paper makes clear his desperate conviction as of late 1933 and early 1934: that he and Zelda were engaged in a battle for survival that only one of them could win. To a considerable extent, both of them moderated this adversarial position during the last half decade of Fitzgerald's life, when they no longer lived together. Ensconced in Hollywood and involved in a relationship with Sheilah Graham complicated by occasional episodes of drunkenness, Scott nonetheless did his best to support Zelda's ongoing medical care and finance Scottie's prep school and college education, and Zelda sent him appreciative and affectionate letters. When he was writing the final version of *Tender Is the Night*, though, the struggle between them strongly influenced what he had to say about the war between the sexes.

VIII. RECEPTION

Loss of Vision

As Matthew J. Bruccoli asserted in his comprehensive study of the novel's various versions, to maintain that the reader "is not prepared for Dick's crack-up is absurd" (MJB, *Composition* 109). The very purpose of Book Two, Bruccoli commented, was to expose Diver's weaknesses of character—his overweening desire to please, above all, but also his susceptibility to drink, to the attractions of young women, and to the power of wealth. And his eventual defeat was predicated in the last pages of Book One as well, during and after the shooting at the Gare St. Lazare. As with most such stories of loss and "unsuccess," the great theme of Fitzgerald's fiction, it is difficult to pinpoint the exact time and place of such a change. "He had lost himself—he could not tell the hour when, or the day or the week, the month or the year," Fitzgerald wrote of his protagonist. "Between the time he found Nicole flowering under a stone on the Zürichsee and the moment of his meeting with Rosemary the spear had been blunted" (229), his weaponry compromised.

Nonetheless, several early reviewers and commentators were troubled by what seemed to them insufficient preparation for Diver's disintegration. As Fitzgerald's mentor at Princeton, Dean Christian Gauss, wrote him after reading the novel in serial form, he felt "that Dick went haywire too fast" (SD, "History" 197). Fitzgerald took these criticisms seriously, and in his notes began to reshape the novel, telling the story chronologically instead of beginning with Rosemary's adoring point of view. These notes formed the basis for the revised edition of *Tender Is the Night* that Malcolm Cowley put together in 1951, a version that has lost favor with both critics and general readers over time.

Most of the problem, I believe, derives from readers so identifying with Dick as to suffer emotional distress at his downfall. Grenberg locates the point of intersection at which the ascending arc of Nicole's growing strength crosses the descending path of Dick's waning energy: in 1925, after six years of marriage (Grenberg 123). Franz had been right, of course, and Diver had suffered along with his wife through her long relapse after daughter Topsy's birth, at first tending to identify with Nicole's pain, and then toughening himself against it, so that it became "difficult to distinguish between his self-protective professional detachment and some new coldness in his heart" (192-93). This double view of her, that of the husband and the psychiatrist, has the effect of "disarming" him (215). Nor could he compete against the sheer force of money working against him.

Tender owes much of its emotional power to its authenticity. The novel records Fitzgerald's "own experience of struggle and heartbreak . . . it rings absolutely true, because it is true" (Scribner ix). Nowhere is its fidelity to the author's own experience more powerfully evident than in the account of Diver's drunken argument with Roman cab drivers and his beating by the police. In the aftermath of Zelda's affair with Edouard Jozan and with Scott virtually finished with *The Great Gatsby*, Zelda was inspired by her reading of Henry James's *Roderick Hudson* to settle in Rome and Capri for the winter of 1924-25. It was not a happy time. In Rome "we were dismal," Scott wrote, and in Capri, Zelda was sick "from trying to have a baby" and "there seemed to be nothing left of happiness in the world" (MJB, *Grandeur* 297). Nor did he get along with the Italians. In "The High Cost of Macaroni," an article intended for the *Saturday Evening Post* that his agent Harold Ober was unable to sell, he inveighed against the social pretensions of the Roman nobility. But he left out the cab driver dispute and his subsequent beating, saving that incident for use in his fiction.

To be sure, much about that night in Rome in *Tender Is the Night* was invented—in particular, the intervention of Baby Warren (a character to some extent based on Gerald Murphy's Anglophilic sister Esther) to rescue her brother-in-law from incarceration. But the quarrel with the cab drivers and the beating by the police were absolutely real. In fact, as Fitzgerald put it in a letter to journalist-novelist Howard (Hungry) Coxe in April 1934, it constituted "just about the rottenest thing that ever happened to me in my life." He'd "gone through hell on that occasion," and though he was "often groggy" about recalling the details "through the dim mist of blood," he did remember that Coxe as well as Zelda helped him get out of jail (FSF, *Correspondence* 349).

Dick's beating, as John Irwin points out, represented only a small part of the process Fitzgerald undertook of "translating" his humiliation and sense of personal deterioration into the depiction of Dick Diver. Moreover, he made this process do double duty in the "Crack-Up" memoir essays of 1936 where, denying an alcoholic origin for his troubles, Fitzgerald acknowledged the same problems in his own life that beset his protagonist in *Tender Is the Night*: "a weariness of people, an inability to participate in routine human relationships, irrational antipathies, and a mounting bigotry" (Irwin 123-24). Above all, both the author and his character suffer from a loss of vitality.

The worst of the physical injuries Diver sustained in Rome was to his eye. Perhaps in order to enlist Baby's determination to liberate him from jail, he initially exaggerates the severity of his wounds. Responding to his cries, Baby manages to locate Dick in the guard room where he's being held. "They've put out my eye," he tells her. "They handcuffed me and then they beat me." Armed with this (mis)information, she hurries to the American embassy— it's still early morning—and tries to use her formidable presence and social and financial position to command the embassy's support. They have to do something, she insists. "They've put out a man's eye—my brother-in-law, and they won't let him out of jail" (258-59).

In an excellent essay, "An 'Unblinding of Eyes': The Narrative Vision of *Tender Is the Night*," Laura Rattray focuses on Diver's loss of vision as the novel proceeds, with the beating in Rome a climactic event. In the opening passages of the novel, Dick is the visual master. His "bright, hard blue eyes" take in the beach scenes with clarity despite the dazzling sun, and—this is more important—he bestows his entire attention on anyone he is talking to, looking at them directly, not merely "glanc[ing]" in their direction. But "[a]s the narrative progresses," Rattray points out, Dick "begins to lose his sight." In Paris he relies on his pince-nez to read, and by the time of the Roman misadventure, he is dependent on spectacles. His visual decline is thus documented as being well underway before the beating in the police station and the "blinding" of eyes that cause his failures of understanding during the dreadful encounters of Book Three (Rattray 89-91).

At the Minghettis and on Golding's yacht, Dick's physical loss of vision is accompanied by a still more debilitating psychological lack of perception. Meanwhile, Nicole is transformed by her own "unblinding" and developing powers to replace her husband and physician as the novel's watcher and seer. The last third of *Tender Is the Night*, Fitzgerald reminded himself as he started writing it in 1932, was to be told "as much as possible through Nicole's eyes" (Rattray 98-99). In the final three-way confrontation with Tommy, Dick refuses to be drawn into a row: "There's less chance of unpleasantness if we avoid a three-cornered discussion." Then he walks away alone, Nicole's "white crook's eyes" following him as he fades into just another dot in the summer crowd (347). Similarly, Fitzgerald's narrator, rarely out of the picture earlier, vanishes from sight, giving way to her vision, her judgments, her interpretations. Yet that narrator, perhaps, deserves the last word on this subject. The marks of suffering, he comments in the middle of Book Two, leave wounds that stay with us forever, comparable "to the loss of a finger or the sight of an eye. We may not miss them . . . for one minute in a year, but if we should there is nothing to be done about it" (193).

Evaluations

Almost inevitably, readers of Fitzgerald's fiction are driven to compare *Tender Is the Night* and *The Great Gatsby*, his two wonderful and very different novels published nine years apart. *Gatsby* is of course more widely recognized among the greatest works of fiction. In a highly publicized poll of the best novels of the twentieth century, Fitzgerald's *Gatsby* came in second only to Joyce's *Ulysses*—a fact that has inspired me to ask lecture audiences to raise their hands to signify whether they have actually read these books. Invariably, far more hands go up for *Gatsby* than for *Ulysses*, and the same result would have come from a show of hands for *Gatsby* vs. *Tender*, inasmuch as the earlier and shorter novel has become a staple reading assignment in secondary school and college English classes.

Fitzgerald has told us in just what terms the two books should be differentiated. "The dramatic novel has canons quite different from the philosophical, now called psychological, novel," he wrote to John Peale Bishop on 7 April 1934, a few days before *Tender* was published. "One is a kind of *tour de force*. It would be like comparing a sonnet sequence with an epic" (FSF, *Life in Letters* 255). His dramatic novel, *Gatsby*, was his *tour de force*, his sonnet sequence, emotionally charged and tightly knit. His psychological novel, *Tender*, was his epic, larger in scope and placing the downfall of its protagonist in a wider social context.

Yet there were obvious parallels between the two novels as well, most obviously the victory of the very rich and defeat of the relatively poor in the fortunes of love. The basic theme, in both books, was characteristically that of loss—lost illusions, lost dreams, lost ideals—as is true of almost all of Fitzgerald's greatest fiction. Yet in *Tender*, the repeated beatings Dick Diver suffers in his battle with Nicole Warren leave one in a state of tremendous emotional pain, and paradoxical though it may seem, the distress the novel leaves behind is what makes it great.

How great will depend, as is true of any literary accomplishment, on the sensitivities of the reader who sits in judgment. Most of the early commentators admired *Tender*, especially Fitzgerald's fellow authors. Bishop himself wrote Fitzgerald that the novel surpassed *Gatsby* and established him as "a true, a beautiful and a tragic novelist." John O'Hara praised it as "one of the great books of the world." Marjorie Kinnan Rawlings, a fellow Scribner (and Max Perkins) novelist, found it "disturbing, bitter, and beautiful," though she felt "totally unable to analyze the almost overpowering effect that some of [Fitzgerald's] passages create" (Scribner xiii). Upon their first meeting, the talented Dorothy Parker and British writer G. B. (Gladys Bronwyn) Stern got to talking about *Tender*. Later Stern wrote Fitzgerald "what a magnificent piece of work it was ... and how it turned us inside out when we read it and didn't put us back again and what lovely sensitive writing was in it" (SD, "Scott and Dottie" 59).

There were some dissenting voices, however. *Tender* was published at the bottom of the Depression, and proletarian critics criticized the book for its subject matter. In his *Daily Worker* review, Philip Rahv castigated Fitzgerald for glamorizing the rich, endowing its members with "a certain grace" and hiding their careless cruelty under cover of a "beach umbrella" (Rahv 7). John Dos Passos offered a useful corrective to that view, lauding Fitzgerald for first presenting a handsome portrait of a dying class and then uncovering the rottenness eating away at it underneath. "The whole conception of the book [the collapse of one of the great postwar imperial delusions] is enormous ... the way you first lay in the pretty picture and then start digging under the surface is immense" (Dos Passos 358). For that reason as well, Dos Passos disagreed with reviewers who thought the book poorly structured by beginning with Rosemary's adoring point of view and hence producing a "categorical expectancy" that Diver must succeed. He had been "enormously thrown off by the beginning," too, only to realize later how well it worked. "It's so tightly knit together that it can't be read in pieces" (359).

Nonetheless, Fitzgerald was troubled by the charge of structural error and by the accompanying assertion, from novelist Joseph Hergesheimer, that it was "almost impossible to write a book about an actress" (SD, "History" 188, 196-97). So, in 1938, he began the process of reshaping *Tender* to start with its "*true* beginning—the young psychiatrist in Switzerland." He cut pages loose from the binding and reassembled them to conform to this different arrangement. But he soon realized that the changed approach would require considerable fine-tuning and made only a few brief but significant revisions, signaling near the end of chapter 2 that he had only progressed that far in making "final corrections" (SD, "History" 200-201). That was the unfinished script that Malcolm Cowley worked with in constructing the 1951 version of *Tender*, beginning with Diver at Dohmler's clinic.

Heartening though the early responses from Bishop, Dos Passos, O'Hara, his longtime admirer Gilbert Seldes, and others may have been, Fitzgerald waited anxiously for word from Hemingway. "Do you like the book?" he wrote Hemingway on 10 May 1934. "For God's sake drop me a line and tell me one way or another." Nothing Ernest said could hurt his feelings, he insisted (FSF, *Life in Letters* 259). Perhaps not, but Hemingway's reply, finding fault with the novel and its author, certainly tested that assertion. For one thing, Hemingway objected to the composite characterizations Fitzgerald used, particularly that of Gerald Murphy-Fitzgerald-Diver. The novel proved that Fitzgerald could think, Hemingway conceded, but he accused him of having stopped listening to others a long time ago, and not listening had a way of drying writers up.

Also, and most of all, Hemingway disapproved of his fellow author's tendency to lament his own troubles in print. (Ernest was to feel the same way, except more so, about Scott's "Crack-Up" essays in *Esquire*.) "Forget your personal tragedy," he instructed Fitzgerald. "We are all bitched from the start and you especially need to be hurt like hell before you can write seriously." It was unfortunate that he had married a woman who wanted to compete with him and "ruin" him, and that he was a "rummy" to boot, but that did not qualify him as "a tragic character." They were both writers, Hemingway lectured him, and what they should do was write. Fitzgerald could write now better than ever, he ended by way of encouragement.

Hemingway's criticisms manifestly had less to do with Fitzgerald's novel than with what he regarded as the waste of his talent. And before long he changed his mind. It was a "strange thing," he wrote Max Perkins on 15 April 1935, that "in retrospect his Tender Is the Night gets better and better. I wish you would tell him I said so" (SD, "History" 197-98). In the short term, then, Hemingway's favorable reevaluation of *Tender* predicted its long-term reputation. It is a novel that has grown "better and better" over time, and with successive readings.

Fitzgerald's literary standing was at its nadir at the time of his death. He was memorialized in the *New York Times* obituary as the author of Jazz Age stories of young love—the kind of fiction he could no longer produce in the last of his four decades, and not at all the subject matter of his major novels. But there was a revival in the mid- and late 1940s and early 1950s. The Armed Forces edition of *Gatsby*, issued free to soldiers and sailors, helped create a new market for his work. Edmund Wilson, his Princeton friend, put together a book incorporating the "Crack-Up" essays with laudatory articles from major figures and interesting selections from Fitzgerald's notebooks. Wilson also edited an edition of *The Last Tycoon*, the highly promising but unfinished novel about Hollywood that Fitzgerald was working on during his final years. Malcolm Cowley issued a fine selection of the best short stories in addition to the reorganized version of *Tender*.

Nonetheless, Fitzgerald did not quickly or easily achieve his eventual status as one of the greatest twentieth-century American writers—someone whose works, especially *Gatsby*, became obligatory reading in high school and college, along with novels by Hemingway, Faulkner, and Steinbeck. And *Tender Is the Night* remained undervalued in the literary marketplace for several decades.

Bennett Cerf of Random House and the Modern Library was one of the first publishers to recognize *Tender's* extraordinary poignancy. In a 1934 letter to fellow editor Maxwell Perkins, Cerf described it as "a haunting book" that "reestablishes Fitzgerald . . . way up there among the stars." Cerf also understood why that was true: because of *Tender's* capacity to draw readers into the emotional defeat of its protagonist. "I found the end so distressing that it's been bothering me for two days. Felt I knew Dick Diver personally, and the spectacle of that gal sucking all the insides from him, and then tossing off the empty skin pained me deep down" (MJB, "Cerf's Fan Letter" 229). Cerf, however, did not see fit to include *Tender* in the Modern Library series of outstanding books.

The novel's exquisitely painful ending is by no means merely about Diver's personal decline and fall. As historian Alan Trachtenberg observed, the struggle involved illusion vs. reality, at the very heart of American myth. Diver's traditional values and eagerness to do right are no match for the Warrens' wealth and hardheadedness. "In the final phase of [his] decline, as he more and more just sits and listens, unable to imagine a future, we learn that an incalculable story was telling itself within him" (Trachtenberg 184-85): the story of what might have been, had the illusions he grew up with proved capable of withstanding the power of the "intensely calculated" world that he encounters. Finally, Diver can only survive by passively surrendering, conceding defeat and carrying that untold story with him as he fades into obscurity.

Tender Is the Night is not only, in novelist Malcolm Bradbury's words, "a great psycho-historical portrait of the age," but is also as moving an account of a human being's collapse as has ever been written. Rereading the novel recently for perhaps the tenth time, in the excellent and authoritative Cambridge edition of James L. W. West III, I was carried away by sorrow and sympathy for Fitzgerald's leading character. So were several of the senior— not college-senior but generationally senior—students in the seminar I was then teaching. Like the poet Weldon Kees, we were "enormously moved by the last pages of *Tender* in their compression and as a triumph of dealing with years that are too sad to insist upon." The book, as Kees wrote, is "soaked" in the tragic sense of life.

I'll share the last word with the critic John Irwin, whose final book was a brilliant study of the theatricality pervading Fitzgerald's fiction. "A work's power to break one's heart," Irwin concluded, constituted one criterion for judging greatness in literary art (Irwin x). By that standard, and it is a sound one, like Irwin I can think of nothing that ranks above *Tender Is the Night*.

WORKS CITED AND CONSULTED

A shorter version of "War and Its Practitioners" was delivered on 7 November 2013 as a keynote talk at the Twelfth Biennial F. Scott Fitzgerald Conference in Montgomery, Alabama. Other material is drawn from two of my published essays: "The Seduction of Doctor Diver," *Hopkins Review* 8, no. 1 (2015): 5-21, and "A Short History of *Tender Is the Night*," in *Writing the American Classics*, edited by James Barbour and Tom Quirk (Chapel Hill: U of North Carolina P, 1990), 177-208.

Benchley, Robert. Letter to F. Scott Fitzgerald, 29 April 1934. F. Scott Fitzgerald Papers, Princeton University Library, Scrapbook 5, p. 7.

Berret, Anthony J. E-mail to author, 13 November 2013.

Blazek, William. "The War Veteran in *Tender Is the Night*." *Back to Peace: Reconciliation and Retribution in the Postwar Period.* Edited by Aranzazu Usandigaza and Andrew Monnickendam. South Bend: Notre Dame UP, 2007. 38-58.

Brown, David S. *Paradise Lost: A Life of Scott Fitzgerald.* Cambridge, MA: Harvard UP, 2017.

Bruccoli, Matthew J. "Bennett Cerf's Fan Letter on *Tender Is the Night*: A Source for Abe North's Death." *Fitzgerald-Hemingway Annual 1979.* Edited by Matthew J. Bruccoli and Richard Layman. Detroit: Gale Research, 1980. 229-30.

———. *The Composition of "Tender Is the Night": A Study of the Manuscripts.* Pittsburgh: U of Pittsburgh P, 1963.

———. *Some Sort of Epic Grandeur: The Life of F. Scott Fitzgerald.* New York: Harcourt Brace Jovanovich, 1981.

Bruccoli, Matthew J., and George Parker Anderson, eds. *F. Scott Fitzgerald's "Tender Is the Night": A Documentary Volume.* Detroit: Bruccoli Clark Layman/Thompson Gale, 2003.

Bruccoli, Matthew J., with Judith S. Baughman. *Reader's Companion to F. Scott Fitzgerald's "Tender Is the Night."* Columbia, SC: U of South Carolina P, 1996.

Donaldson, Scott. *Fool for Love: F. Scott Fitzgerald.* New York: Congdon and Weed, 1983.

———. *Hemingway vs. Fitzgerald: The Rise and Fall of a Literary Friendship.* New York: Overlook Press, 1999.

———. "The Political Development of F. Scott Fitzgerald." *Prospects* 6 (1981): 313-55.

———. "Scott and Dottie." *Sewanee Review* 124 (Winter 2016): 40-61.

———. "The Seduction of Dr. Diver." *Hopkins Review* 8, no.1 (2015): 5-21.

———. "A Short History of *Tender Is the Night.*" *Writing the American Classics.* Edited by James Barbour and Tom Quirk. Chapel Hill: U of North Carolina P, 1990. 177-208.

Dos Passos, John. Letter to F. Scott Fitzgerald, ca. April 1934. F. Scott Fitzgerald, *Correspondence of F. Scott Fitzgerald.* Edited by Matthew J. Bruccoli and Margaret M. Duggan. New York: Random House, 1980. 358-59.

Fitzgerald, F. Scott. *Correspondence of F. Scott Fitzgerald.* Edited by Matthew J. Bruccoli and Margaret M. Duggan. New York: Random House, 1980.

———. "The Death of My Father." *A Short Autobiography.* Edited by James L. W. West III. New York: Scribner, 2011. 118-20.

———. *F. Scott Fitzgerald: A Life in Letters.* Edited by Matthew J. Bruccoli. New York: Simon and Schuster, 1994.

———. *F. Scott Fitzgerald's Ledger: A Facsimile.* Edited by Matthew J. Bruccoli. Washington, DC: Bruccoli Clark/NCR Microcard Editions, 1972.

———. *The Great Gatsby: An Edition of the Manuscript.* Edited by James L. W. West III and Don C. Skemer. New York: Cambridge UP, 2018.

———. *The Letters of F. Scott Fitzgerald.* Edited by Andrew Turnbull. New York: Scribner, 1963.

———. *My Lost City.* Edited by James L. W. West III. New York: Cambridge UP, 2005.

———. *Tender Is the Night: A Romance.* New York: Scribner, 1934.

———. *Tender Is the Night: A Romance.* Preface by Malcolm Cowley. Appendix "Wanda Breasted." New York: Scribner, 1951.

———. *Tender Is the Night: A Romance.* Edited by James L. W. West III. New York: Scribner, 2012.

Fitzgerald, F. Scott, and Zelda Fitzgerald. *Bits of Paradise: 21 Uncollected Stories by F. Scott and Zelda Fitzgerald.* Edited with a preface by Matthew J. Bruccoli. Foreword by Scottie Fitzgerald Smith. New York: Scribner, 1973.

———. *Dear Scott, Dearest Zelda: The Love Letters of F. Scott and Zelda Fitzgerald.* Edited by Jackson R. Bryer and Cathy W. Barks. New York: St. Martin's, 2002.

Fitzgerald, F. Scott, and Maxwell Perkins. *Dear Scott / Dear Max: The Fitzgerald-Perkins Correspondence.* Edited by John Kuehl and Jackson R. Bryer. New York: Scribner, 1971.

Fitzgerald, Zelda. *Save Me the Waltz.* London: Jonathan Cape, 1968.

Garrett, George. "Fire and Freshness: A Matter of Style." *New Essays on The Great Gatsby.* Edited by Matthew J. Bruccoli. New York: Cambridge UP, 1985. 101-16.

Grenberg, Bruce L. "Fitzgerald's 'Figured Curtain': Personality and History in

Tender Is the Night." *Fitzgerald/
Hemingway Annual 1978.* Edited by
Matthew J. Bruccoli and Richard
Layman. Detroit: Gale Research, 1979.
105-36. Reprint, Stern, *Critical Essays,*
211-37.

Hemingway, Ernest. *The Letters of Ernest
Hemingway.* Vol. 2 (1923–1925). Edited
by Sandra Spanier et al. New York:
Cambridge UP, 2013.

———. *A Moveable Feast.* New York: Scribner,
1964.

Irwin, John T. *F. Scott Fitzgerald's Fiction: "An
Almost Theatrical Innocence."* Baltimore:
Johns Hopkins UP, 2014.

Joseph, Tiffany. "'Non-Combatant's Shell-
Shock': Trauma and Gender in F. Scott
Fitzgerald's *Tender Is the Night.*" *NWSA
Journal* 15, no. 3 (2003): 64-81.

Menand, Louis. "Inside the Billway." *New York
Review of Books,* 14 August 1997.

Piper, Henry Dan. *F. Scott Fitzgerald: A Critical
Portrait.* New York: Holt, Rinehart and
Winston, 1965.

Rahv, Philip. "You Can't Duck Hurricane Under
a Beach Umbrella." *Daily Worker,* 5 May
1934, 7.

Rattray, Laura. "An 'Unblinding of Eyes': The
Narrative Vision of *Tender Is the Night.*"
*Twenty-First Century Readings of Tender
Is the Night.* Edited by William Blazek
and Laura Rattray. Liverpool: Liverpool
UP, 2007. 85-102.

Rennie, David. "'The World Only Exists
Through Your Apprehension': World
War I in *This Side of Paradise* and *Tender
Is the Night.*" *F. Scott Fitzgerald Review* 14
(2016): 181-97.

Scribner, Charles, III. Introduction to F. Scott
Fitzgerald, *Tender Is the Night.* New
York: Scribner, 1995. ix-xv.

Sklar, Robert. *F. Scott Fitzgerald: The Last
Laocoön.* New York: Oxford UP, 1967.

Spicer, Paul. "The Shooting at the Gare du
Nord." *Vanity Fair,* 16 July 2010. Excerpt
from Spicer's *The Temptress.* New York:
St. Martin's, 2010.

Stern, Milton R., ed. *Critical Essays on F. Scott
Fitzgerald's "Tender Is the Night."* Boston:
G. K. Hall, 1986. Introduction, 25-30.

———. "*Tender Is the Night* and American
History." *Cambridge Companion to F.
Scott Fitzgerald.* Edited by Ruth Prigozy.
New York: Cambridge UP, 2002. 95-117.

———. *Tender Is the Night: The Broken Universe.*
New York: Twayne, 1994.

Trachtenberg, Alan. "The Journey Back: Myth
and History in *Tender Is the Night.*" Stern,
Critical Essays, 170-85.

Tuttleton, James W. "Vitality and Vampirism in
Tender Is the Night." Stern, *Critical Essays,*
238-46.

West, Suzanne. "Nicole's Gardens." *Fitzgerald/
Hemingway Annual 1978.* Edited by
Matthew J. Bruccoli and Richard
Layman. Detroit: Gale Research, 1979.
85-96.

Wilson, Edmund. "A Weekend at Ellerslie." *The
Shores of Light.* New York: Farrar, Straus
and Young, 1952. 373-83.

TWO

Gatsby and the American Dream

In an evaluation of the greatest novels of the twentieth century, F. Scott Fitzgerald's *The Great Gatsby* came in second, behind James Joyce's *Ulysses*. The single greatest difference between the two may be that everyone has read *Gatsby*, but *Ulysses*, not so much.

Fitzgerald had a number of other titles in mind, including *Trimalchio*, which he used in the semi-final draft. Trimalchio, a character in *The Satyricon* by Petronius, is not to the manner born, but through hard work and perseverance manages to attain wealth and power. To call attention to himself, he throws lavish dinner parties where the liquor flows and the guests behave— like those at Gatsby's mansion—like people at amusement parks.

Fitzgerald switched the title to *The Great Gatsby*, realizing that calling his book *Trimalchio* would place his leading character in too unpleasant a light. It's true that Nick Carraway, the narrator of the book, says that he disapproved of Gatsby from beginning to end, yet near that end he comes to admire this arriviste for the sheer magnitude and persistence of his dreams and to tell him that he's worth more than the whole damn bunch of Tom and Daisy Buchanans and Jordan Bakers put together. Using Nick to tell the story was a masterstroke, for he is, to put the matter baldly, a snob, and it was not easy for a snob like Nick to let his latent idealism emerge and come to admire Jimmy Gatz.

The Great Gatsby tells a singularly American story of the rise to riches. But this is not Horatio Alger, where Mark the Match Boy rescues the tycoon's daughter from a runaway horse-carriage and subsequently marries the girl, takes over the business, and lives happily ever after. If you measure success by the customary US standards of fame and money, Fitzgerald's lower-middle-class boy who grows up on the shores of Lake Superior and goes off to reinvent himself is certainly successful. Yet he fails to capture Daisy, and Fitzgerald's novel shows us why.

When T. S. Eliot wrote Fitzgerald that *Gatsby* seemed to him "the first step that American fiction has taken since Henry James," he linked the two writers as *social* novelists in whose work the issue is joined between innocence and experience, between those who repudiate artificial limitations and those who recognize and respect what James called "the envelope of circumstances," between the individual yearning for independence and the society forever reining him in. Fitzgerald, like James, understood that this pursuit of independence was doomed from the start.

One's house, one's clothes: they do express one's self, and for no one more than Jay Gatsby. It is in good part because of the clothes he wears that Tom Buchanan is able to undermine him as a competitor for Daisy. "An Oxford man!" says Tom. "Like hell he is! He wears a pink suit." Yes, and for tea a white flannel suit with silver shirt and gold tie. And drives a monstrously long cream-colored car, a veritable "circus wagon," in Tom's damning phrase. And inhabits a huge mansion where he throws drunken parties "for the world and its mistress." Gatsby's clothes, his car, his house, his parties—all brand him as newly rich, unschooled in the social graces and casual sense of superiority ingrained in those brought up in an atmosphere of privilege.

Jay Gatsby's fate is predicted by what happens to Myrtle Wilson. Married to the pallid proprietor of a gas station in the ash heaps, Myrtle must cross a vast social divide to reach the territory of the upper class. Her sensuality enables her to attract Tom Buchanan, and in the small apartment on West 158th Street that Tom rents as a place of assignation, she pitifully attempts to put on airs. Yet what Myrtle buys and plans to buy during the Sunday party in chapter 2 tellingly reveals her status. She aims for extravagance but has had no experience with it.

When Myrtle and Tom and Nick Carraway, who has been commandeered by Tom to "meet his girl," reach Grand Central Station, Myrtle buys a copy of the gossip magazine *Town Tattle* at the newsstand and "some cold cream and a small flask of perfume" from the drugstore's cosmetics counter. These were not purchases Daisy Buchanan would have made. Next, Myrtle exercises her discrimination by letting several taxicabs go by before selecting a lavender-colored one—not quite a circus wagon, but unseemly in its showy color. Then she stops the cab in order to "get one of those dogs" for the apartment from a sidewalk salesman. This man resembles John D. Rockefeller and is, like him, less than straightforward in his business dealings. He claims that the puppy he fetches from his basket is a male Airedale and demands ten dollars for it. In fact, the dog is a mongrel bitch, and in a gesture Myrtle must have found wonderfully cavalier, Tom pays the inflated price with a characteristic insult. "Here's your money. Go and buy ten more dogs with it."

Later that day, Myrtle puts together a shopping list that includes a "massage and a wave and a collar for the dog and one of those cute little ashtrays where you touch a spring, and a wreath with a black silk bow" for her mother's grave. "I got to write down a list so I won't forget all the things I got to do," she announces. The "I got" idiom betrays her humble origins, and the list itself, with its emphasis on ashes and dust, foreshadows her demise.

Among Myrtle's purchases, the dog of indeterminate breeding best symbolizes her situation. She is, for Tom, a possession to be played with, fondled, and in due course abandoned. For the times, Tom was not unusual in regarding women as objects to be possessed—either temporarily, as in the case of Myrtle, or permanently, if like Daisy they warranted such maintenance through their beauty and background and way of presenting themselves. Tom does not actually dismiss Myrtle in the course of the novel—indeed, he seems to be trying to continue the affair—but there is no question that she would eventually be discarded, like the Santa Barbara chambermaid he was discovered with shortly after his marriage to Daisy, or the woman who caused the trouble in Chicago, or for that matter the office girl Nick relinquishes after her brother begins casting dark looks at him. It does not come to that, for Myrtle dies when struck by Gatsby's car, Daisy at the wheel.

Jay Gatsby, son of Henry C. Gatz before he reimagines himself into a son of God, has risen from much the same social stratum as Myrtle Wilson. The limitations of this background finally make it impossible for him to win the enduring love of Daisy Fay Buchanan. And, like Myrtle, he is guilty of a crucial error in judgment. They are both unwilling or unable to comprehend that it is not money alone that matters, but money combined with secure social position.

In depicting the unhappy end of Myrtle Wilson and Jay Gatsby, Fitzgerald was painting a broad-brush portrait of his own experience. Near the end of the novel, Nick condemns Tom and Daisy as careless people who "smashed up things and creatures and then retreated back into their money or their vast carelessness or whatever it was that kept them together." In this bitter passage, Fitzgerald was writing about himself as well as the characters. "The whole idea of Gatsby," as he put it, "is the unfairness of a poor young man not being able to marry a girl with money. The theme comes up again and again because I lived it." Lived it with Ginevra King, the Lake Forest debutante who serves as the principal model for Daisy, and very nearly again with Zelda Sayre.

In rejecting Scott as a suitor, Ginevra made it painfully clear that there were boundaries he could not cross. When he visited her in Lake Forest, the exurban enclave which Fitzgerald at twenty thought the most glamorous place in the world, Ginevra's father made a remark—"poor boys shouldn't think of marrying rich girls," he said—that Fitzgerald took to heart as directed toward him and never forgot.

Nor, as *The Great Gatsby* demonstrates, can money itself buy the love of the rich girl, or certainly not the tainted money Gatsby accumulates in his campaign to take Daisy away from her husband. It would have been difficult for him to compete with Tom's resources, in any event. Nick describes the Buchanans as "enormously wealthy" and Tom himself as notorious for reckless spending. When he and Daisy moved from Lake Forest to East Egg (on the north shore of Long Island), he brought along a string of polo ponies. "It was hard to realize that a man in my own generation was wealthy enough to do that," Nick observes.

Part of Gatsby's dream is to turn back the clock and marry Daisy in a conventional wedding, but there too he would have been hard put to equal Tom's extravagance. When Tom married Daisy in June 1919, he brought with him a hundred guests in four private railway cars. It took an entire floor of the hotel to put them up. As a wedding gift, he presented Daisy with "a string of pearls valued at three hundred and fifty thousand dollars"—an impressive sum in 1919 (or any other time), but nonetheless marked down from "seven hundred and fifty thousand dollars" in *Trimalchio*, the version of the novel Fitzgerald sent Maxwell Perkins in the fall of 1924. Fitzgerald must have decided that the higher figure was beyond belief.

Even discounting how much there is of it, Tom's "old money" has a power beyond any Gatsby can command. Tom's wealth and background win the battle for Daisy, despite his habitual infidelities—an outcome that seems not only grossly unfair but morally wrong, for another point Fitzgerald is making is that if you have enough money and position you can purchase immunity from punishment. Actions have consequences, we remind our children, but some people can evade those consequences. Gatsby himself probably avoids prosecution for bootlegging and bond-rigging by distributing his resources on a *quid pro quo* basis, and he rather callously applies that principle to his personal life as well. Once he did the police commissioner a favor. Now he can break the speed limit. Nick arranges a meeting with Daisy. Gatsby offers him a business connection.

Gatsby's evasions, however, are as nothing compared to those of the Buchanans. Daisy commits vehicular manslaughter, then compounds the felony by letting others think Gatsby was driving. In directing Wilson to West Egg, Tom escapes the wrath he knows should be directed at him and becomes an accessory to murder. The message would seem to be that if you have the right background, you can get away with murder. In *Gatsby* itself, the two characters who fall in love above their station pay with their lives for their presumption, while Tom and Daisy assuage any discomfort they may feel over cold chicken and ale. Get mixed up with the Buchanans, and you end up dead.

Fitzgerald's detestation of the plutocracy is powerfully evoked in this novel, as it is in *Tender Is the Night*, and again the sentiment derived from his own experience. In "The Crack-Up," written in 1936, Fitzgerald ruefully recounted the reluctance of Zelda Sayre to marry him just after World War I, when his prospects as a husband and provider looked mighty bleak. To win her over, he rewrote his first novel, *This Side of Paradise*, and had it accepted, but the process changed him. Thereafter he cherished "an abiding distrust, an animosity, toward the leisure class—not the conviction of the revolution-ist but the smoldering hatred of the peasant. In the years since then I have never been able to stop wondering where my friends' money came from, nor to stop thinking that at one time a sort of *droit du seigneur* might have been exercised to give one of them my girl."

The ideas of Thorstein Veblen, a social commentator of wide influence, are closely reflected in Fitzgerald's novel. In his *Theory of the Leisure Class* (1899), Veblen advanced three basic ideas that he called "Pecuniary Emula-tion," "Conspicuous Leisure," and—in a phrase that quickly became part of the language—"Conspicuous Consumption." All three are vividly illustrated in the pages of *The Great Gatsby*. In an industrial society, Veblen argued, accumulated property replaced "trophies of predatory exploit" as a sign of potency. In order to establish his worth and earn the esteem of others, one had to achieve economic success—and to show it. The competition to rival the very rich required acquisition of material goods in order to create "an invidious comparison" between oneself and those less successful. Veblen called this process "pecuniary emulation," and he judged it to have become the primary motive for the accumulation of wealth.

According to this theory, one might suppose that Jay Gatsby could realize his dream by making a fortune and putting it on display. But Veblen added an important caveat: that inherited wealth was "even *more* honorific" than that acquired through one's own efforts. In fact, only those with inherited money could live a life of leisure naturally and comfortably, for they inherited gentility along with their wealth, and "with the inheritance of gentility goes the inheritance of obligatory leisure." If you were born into this leisure class, you were virtually obliged to abstain "from productive work." Nick comes from a genteel background, but the family money has evaporated and he must find a socially approved occupation—the bond business—to support himself. Gatsby has all the money he could possibly need and ostentatiously presents it for public view, but he cannot acquire the social stature that comes with inherited wealth. Only Tom qualifies as a fully validated member of the new leisure class.

In a culture where pecuniary emulation predominates, the single most important object by which to declare one's status is the house. In *The Great Gatsby* Fitzgerald masterfully discriminates between Tom Buchanan and Jay Gatsby, the rivals for Daisy's love, on the basis of the very different homes they occupy on Long Island. And houses serve to define Nick and Daisy as well.

Though he lacks the Buchanans' financial resources, Nick shares their privileged background. At Yale, for instance, he belonged to the same senior society as Tom, and few organizations are more selective than Yale senior societies. During the course of the novel, Nick lives for eighty dollars a month in a weather-beaten cardboard bungalow "squeezed between two huge places that rented for twelve or fifteen thousand a season"—at least fifty times as much as Nick was paying. But after the disastrous summer of 1922 he can safely return to the "Carraway house" in the midwestern city—Fitzgerald's St. Paul, surely—where his "well-to-do, prominent" family had lived for three generations.

In Louisville, similarly, Daisy grew up in the Fay house. Gatsby meets her there in 1917, when red, white, and blue banners patriotically whipped in the summer wind: "The largest of the banners and the largest of the lawns belonged to Daisy Fay's house." The place entirely enchants the poor young officer, as does Daisy herself, the golden girl dressed in white, driving her white roadster, living in a white palace. In Gatsby's imagination, Daisy and her house are inseparable, while she comfortably changes location from the white palace in Louisville to an elegant home in Lake Forest, and finally to the mansion Tom buys for her among the "palaces of fashionable East Egg," a magical place where nature is harnessed for the pleasure of its inhabitants.

Even the Buchanans' lawn has miraculous qualities. On its course up from the beach, it runs for a quarter mile, jumps over sundials and brick walls, drifts up the outside wall, and even seems to grow a little way inside the house itself. A breeze blows through a rosy-colored room from French windows ajar at either end, and there on an enormous couch repose Daisy Buchanan and Jordan Baker in their white dresses. The two young women are "buoyed up" on the couch "as though upon an anchored balloon." Their dresses ripple in the breeze, as if they had just returned from a short flight. Then Tom shuts the rear windows, cutting off the wind, and they balloon slowly to the floor.

When Nick comes to dinner there, the decorum of the evening is shattered by Myrtle's inopportune phone calls, and in an effort to change the subject, Tom proposes taking Nick down to see the stables. The subject comes up again on Nick's next visit to the Buchanans, during the climactic and stifling Sunday afternoon. On this occasion Daisy and Jordan are again dressed in white and are lying on an enormous couch, but they are weighted down like "silver idols" in the heat of the day, with the awnings drawn.

Despite the oppressive weather, Tom proclaims his legerdemain. A few pages earlier, Gatsby had his famous conversation with Nick about the passage of time. "Can't repeat the past?" he says. "Why of course you can." Gatsby will discover that he cannot, while it is Tom who manages to turn back the pages of the calendar. "I've heard of making a garage out of a stable," Tom tells Gatsby, "but I'm the first man who ever made a stable out of a garage."

As Tom and Nick and Jordan drive back from the city later that day, the Buchanans' home, contravening gravity, comes floating "suddenly toward them through the dark, rustling trees," two windows on the second floor abloom with light. Against such violations of natural law, Gatsby can hardly compete. To be sure, his own house, a huge "imitation of some Hotel de Ville in Normandy," looms large. It looks like the World's Fair when all the lights are turned on but remains earthbound throughout.

As Nick comments during Gatsby's first party, in his experience "young men didn't . . . drift coolly out of nowhere and buy a palace on Long Island Sound." Rumors circulate about Gatsby's past: he killed a man; he was a German spy during the war. He spreads some of them himself, as in his recital (for Nick's benefit) of an impossible past that involves hunting tigers and collecting rubies. "I didn't want you to think I was just some nobody," he explains. This phrase finds an echo, in a novel filled with echoes, during the confrontation scene at the Plaza when Tom remarks that he doesn't intend to "sit back and let Mr. Nobody from Nowhere make love to [his] wife." Gatsby's outsized house, together with the parties and the clothing, the automobile and the aquaplane, represent his attempt to establish himself as Somebody, or at least not Nobody.

The trouble is that these possessions, which Gatsby shows off like a peacock, proclaim his inferior social status. Nick describes Gatsby's mansion as "a *colossal* affair by any standard," and it is no accident that he borrows the adjective from the promotional language of motion picture advertisements. Gatsby bought the place, in downscale West Egg, solely because it was situated across the bay from Daisy and so might facilitate a reunion. Despite the undoubted impressiveness of his house, though, Gatsby lacks the kind of confident assurance about it that Tom displays. "My house looks well, doesn't it?" Gatsby *asks* Nick, seeking validation—and misusing the word "well." "I've got a nice place here," Tom *tells* Nick, brooking no dissent.

Gatsby gives Nick and Daisy a tour of his Hotel de Ville, leading them through an architecturally eclectic mishmash. The house contains a bit of everything: Restoration salons and Marie Antoinette music rooms, period bedrooms and an Adam study. Gatsby gives them a glass of Chartreuse from a cupboard in the study, opens two "hulking" cabinets in the bedroom to display the suits and shirts his man in England sends him, and calls on Klipspringer, his "boarder," to play two tellingly inappropriate tunes on the piano—"The Love Nest" and "Ain't We Got Fun?" Daisy professes to "adore" everything and proposes the kind of experiment in transforming nature that seems possible only to the Buchanans of the world. She and Gatsby are standing at the window gazing at pink and golden clouds over the sea. "I'd like to just get one of those clouds," she whispers to him, "and put you in it and push you around."

Gatsby's house is for show, certainly, and so are his parties. When Daisy wonders how he can live there alone, Gatsby says he keeps the place "always full of interesting people. . . . People who do interesting things. Celebrated people." Finally, Daisy and Tom are prevailed upon to come across the bay to one of the parties. The evening does not go well. Gatsby "certainly must have strained himself to get this menagerie together," Tom comments. Daisy defends the assembled crowd—and by extension, Gatsby himself—but without conviction, for she too is appalled by West Egg in general, this place of raw emotions that "Broadway had begotten upon a Long Island fishing village."

The party marks the beginning of the end for Daisy and Gatsby. Daisy didn't have a good time, a discouraged Gatsby tells Nick afterward. Thereupon he ends the parties, fires the servants, lets the place deteriorate. Everything is dusty and in disarray when Nick comes to see Gatsby early in the morning after the disastrous day at the Plaza and the fatal accident on the road. Together they throw open the windows, and Gatsby tells Nick the real story of what he learned from Dan Cody and how he fell in love with Daisy Fay. After they have breakfast together, Nick, fearing the worst, reluctantly takes the train into town. He is still there when George Wilson finds his way to Gatsby's house and pool sometime between two and four in the afternoon.

Assuming responsibility for the funeral arrangements, Nick keeps vigil at Gatsby's house until his father arrives. Henry C. Gatz brings two mementoes of his son for Nick's inspection. One is a boyhood schedule and list of general resolves written on the flyleaf of a Hopalong Cassidy book. This document sets forth an ambitious program for personal improvement reminiscent of Benjamin Franklin's autobiography: "Study needed inventions," "Practice elocution, poise and how to attain it," "No more smokeing or chewing." "It just shows you," Mr. Gatz declares, in a surge of pride for his son's attempt to reimagine himself.

Mr. Gatz's other treasure is a photograph of Gatsby's house, "cracked in the corners and dirty with many hands," which he fishes out of his wallet to show Nick. "Look there," he says, and again, "Look there." He and Nick are standing in the hall of the house, but as far as Mr. Gatz is concerned they might be anywhere. What matters is the soiled photograph in his hands, more real to him than the house itself. "[I]t's a very pretty picture. It shows up well," Mr. Gatz observes. It is appropriate that he should be fixated on a photographic image that seems to freeze time. Father and son alike prefer the imagined to the real, the romantic past to the material present.

On the night before returning to the Middle West, Nick pays a final visit to the "huge incoherent failure of a house" that in its effrontery mirrors Gatsby's own ostentation. Concerned as always with propriety, Nick erases an obscene word some boy had scrawled on the front steps. Then he strolls down to the beach, sprawls on the sand, lets his mind wander in search of a moral. "[A]s the moon rose higher the inessential houses began to melt away"—inessential because inescapably concrete, solid, and substantial, and thus unworthy of the wonder the Dutch sailors felt upon beholding for the first time the "fresh, green breast of the new world," or of Gatsby's wonder when he first picked out the green light at the end of Daisy's dock and stretched out his arms toward a dream that would forever elude his grasp.

This is a moving, even uplifting, conclusion. But *The Great Gatsby* conveys another message as well. It tells a cautionary tale about the debilitating effects of money and class on American society and those who seek fulfillment within its confines. In his fiction Fitzgerald regarded that culture both from within, as someone typical of and essentially involved in it, and from without, as a disinterested and hardheaded observer. From *within* he elicits our emotional involvement in Gatsby's quest. From *without* he shows us the cracks in the glittering surface, the poison eating its way underneath. It is this double vision that makes *The Great Gatsby* a great novel.

THREE

Summer of '24

Zelda's Affair

Scott and Zelda Fitzgerald came to France in May 1924 to get away from the frantic party life in the New York exurbs of Westport and Great Neck. Scott was deteriorating under a regimen of "drinking and raising hell generally," as he wrote Maxwell Perkins (FSF, *Life in Letters* 67). So he and Zelda and baby Scottie went to Europe for a fresh start, where he settled down to write a masterpiece. "[N]ever before," as he was to observe in looking back on that time, did he "keep his artistic conscience as pure as during the ten months" (FSF, *Gatsby* [Modern Library] viii) when he was working on *The Great Gatsby*.

He achieved that novel despite, or perhaps because of, a crisis in his marriage. After a few days in Paris, and a week or two trying this place and that on the Riviera, Zelda and Scott moved into the Villa Marie in Valescure, two and a half kilometers from Saint-Raphaël. It was a beautiful house, set high and cool above the beach, with eucalyptus trees and parasol pines warding off the sun. While Scott immersed himself in the book, Zelda cast about for something to do. "What'll we do with ourselves this afternoon . . . and the day after that, and the next thirty years?" Daisy Buchanan inquires in *The Great Gatsby*. "What'll we *do* . . . with ourselves?" Alabama Knight echoes in Zelda's novel *Save Me the Waltz* (qtd. in LeVot 172-73).

Scottie, not yet two, was under the meticulous care of an English nanny they'd hired in Paris. Servants looked after the house and prepared the meals. With time on her hands, Zelda swam in the Mediterranean, tanned herself to a biscuit brown, and began studying French. In the evenings she tackled the novels of Henry James, while Scott read lives of Byron and Shelley. Still, she was bored, while Scott was happily engrossed in the book he was writing. "We are idyllicly [sic] settled here," he wrote Perkins on 13 June (FSF, *Life in Letters* 76). The idyll would soon be interrupted.

Seeking companions during the long summer days, Zelda met three young French naval aviators on the beach. They were stationed at nearby Fréjus and had rented quarters close to the Fitzgeralds. The four of them played tennis together and took the sun. They chatted as well as they could, Zelda working from her French-English dictionary. After a time, she and one of the officers paired off; in the evenings they sometimes danced together. By midsummer she either did or did not have an affair with this young man, and this led to an emotional crisis.

The facts of the matter are beyond ascertaining. It was more than eighty years ago, and no one alive today was on the scene to observe or testify. What is clear is that whatever happened opened a rift in the Fitzgeralds' marriage that could not easily be mended. Neither Zelda nor Scott tried to hush up the affair. Both of them talked about it, wrote about it, worried it obsessively. It stands as a crucial and complicated chapter in their troubled life story.

The endeavor here is not so much to piece together the truth as to examine what biographers have made of Zelda's affair, or fling, or flirtation. The process may reveal as much about the craft of biography and its practitioners as about the Fitzgeralds themselves and what they did or said they did or imagined they did in the summer of 1924.

THE FRENCH AVIATOR

It took more than thirty years to get the facts straight about the French naval officers who swam into Scott's and Zelda's lives in the summer of 1924. In *The Far Side of Paradise* (1951), Arthur Mizener, Fitzgerald's first biographer, devoted three and a half pages to the affair but did not do much digging. Relying on Scott's *Ledger* and *Notebooks* and Zelda's *Save Me the Waltz* (1932) as sources, Mizener assumed that Zelda and one of the Frenchmen had committed adultery. He was interested almost solely in the effect that this had on Fitzgerald. "Sexual matters were always deadly serious to him," Mizener commented, and "his capacity for being hurt by Zelda was always very great" (Mizener 179).

In a long paragraph that he quoted from *Save Me the Waltz*, Mizener stressed the physical nature of Zelda's lover: a dark, romantic fellow with "broad bronze hands . . . convex shoulders . . . slim and strong and rigid" (Mizener 178). His principal error was to get this man's name wrong. Mizener misidentifies him as René Silvé. One of the Frenchmen the Fitzgeralds came to know was indeed named René Silvy (not Silvé), but Silvy did not have an affair with Zelda Fitzgerald and may very well have been gay.

Eleven years later, in his *Scott Fitzgerald* (1962), Andrew Turnbull substituted another error for Mizener's. Like the previous biographer, Turnbull emphasized how shattered Scott was when he discovered what was going on: "He really believed in love, in what two people can build against the world's cheap skepticism." But Turnbull further speculated on Zelda's motives. "At twenty-three—almost twenty-four—she may have begun to fear that her looks were going, or she may have felt insufficient basking in her husband's glory. Perhaps she was trying to make him jealous, or perhaps she was bored and the seduction of the moment proved too strong."

As to the officer's identity, however, Turnbull remained as mistaken as Mizener. He quoted from "How to Live on Practically Nothing a Year," Scott's magazine article for the *Saturday Evening Post* of 20 September 1924: "[I]n half an hour, René and Bobbé, officers of aviation, are coming to dinner in their white ducks." Then in parenthesis, Turnbull equated "Bobbé" (not René) with Edouard Josanne, a name fetched from Fitzgerald's correspondence with Zelda's psychiatrists in the early 1930s (Turnbull 145). This was wrong, in two ways. There was a Bobbé, all right, and he was probably René's partner, but Scott was not disguising Edouard Josanne as Bobbé. He simply left Josanne out of his lighthearted magazine piece as a complication too painful (or valuable) to be addressed there.

At least Turnbull came close to getting the fellow's name right. "Edouard" was accurate, and "Josanne" was close. That was how Scott spelled his family name (he got Edouard wrong too, leaving out the "o"). For her part, Zelda spelled the name as "Josen." Not until Nancy Milford's *Zelda: A Biography* (1970) would someone spell the name correctly in print. Having located and corresponded with the man, Milford correctly identified him as Edouard Jozan, who went on from youthful indiscretions on the Riviera to a distinguished career in the French navy, winning medals for valor and retiring as an admiral. In a long letter to Milford, Jozan wrote that Zelda was indeed "a shining beauty," and he was attracted to her, but there was no affair. The supposed infidelity was a joint invention of the Fitzgeralds, he thought. "[T]hey both had a need of drama, they made it up and perhaps they were the victims of their own unsettled and a little unhealthy imagination."

Milford backed up this interpretation in an interview with Hadley Hemingway, Ernest's first wife. According to Hadley, Zelda liked to dramatize the supposed affair, going so far as to tell others that her lover killed himself when Scott broke off the relationship. "It was one of their acts together. I remember Zelda's face becoming very, very solemn, and she would say how he had loved her and how hopeless it had been and then how he had committed suicide. Scott would stand next to her looking very pale and distressed and sharing every minute of it" (Milford 108, 112-14).

Ernest Hemingway, unlike Hadley, was inclined to believe that the affair was real. In *A Moveable Feast* (1964), Hemingway wrote that Scott had told him several versions of the story about "something tragic that happened . . . at St.-Raphael. The first version that he told me of Zelda and a French aviator falling in love was truly a sad story and I believe it was a true story." Later versions were better told each time, "but they never hurt you the same way the first one did." Fitzgerald's storytelling was so persuasive, Hemingway wrote, that he could envision the lover's single-seater seaplane buzzing the diving raft "and Zelda's tan and Scott's tan and the dark blonde and the light blond of their hair and the darkly tanned face of the boy that was in love with Zelda" (EH 147-48).

Here two conflicting patterns begin to emerge in biographical treatment of the incident. A majority of the female biographers—with the exception of Kendall Taylor and Linda Wagner-Martin—tend to deny that the affair actually took place and assume that the crisis it generated was more or less fabricated by the Fitzgeralds. Most of the male biographers, with the exception of James Mellow, follow the lead of Mizener and Turnbull in believing that Zelda and Jozan's relationship was indeed adulterous.

A year after Milford's biography, which concentrated for the first time on Zelda and not on her more famous husband, Sara Mayfield published *Exiles from Paradise* (1971). Mayfield, who had grown up with Zelda Sayre in Montgomery, Alabama, adamantly maintained that nothing significant happened between Zelda and Jozan. "[T]heir 'affair' was nothing more than a summer flirtation, romantic, decorous, and slightly comic," she wrote, using *her* interview with Jozan—in which he talks of others' accounts of the summer of '24 as "raving mad" and full of "wild ideas"—to bolster her case (Mayfield 96-97).

In Mayfield's judgment, Scott practiced a double standard in overreacting to this flirtation. "If Zelda's eyes wandered, Scott's pride prompted him to attack her and the man to whom she was attracted; but if Zelda's *amour propre* was wounded by Scott's attentions to other women [including, she says, both *"poules de luxe* and stars of the screen and stage"] she wanted only to destroy herself" (Mayfield 117). If anything, Mayfield demonstrated an even stronger bias against Scott than Milford had. In her account he emerged as something of a tyrant, unable or unwilling to understand and adapt to Zelda's Southern ways.

It remained for André LeVot to establish the background of the three Frenchmen stationed at Fréjus. In *F. Scott Fitzgerald: A Biography* (1983), LeVot fleshes them out as René Silvy, son of a Cannes notary public, a young man with literary ambitions; Bobbé (surname in some doubt, but possibly Croirier), a veteran of World War I who had fought at Verdun and shared a literary bent with René; and of course Edouard Jozan, son of a middle-class family in Nîmes who was about to embark on a fine career in the navy.

Curiously, various biographers presented conflicting accounts about Jozan's hair color. Mizener gave him "curly black hair" (Mizener 178), and Milford described his hair as "dark and curling" (Milford 108), but Mayfield—perhaps relying on Zelda's characterization in *Save Me the Waltz* of a golden-haired lover—cited his "curly blond hair," as did LeVot (Mayfield 97; LeVot 174). Then as late as 1993 Jeffrey Meyers's *Scott Fitzgerald* reverted to Mizener's account of the Frenchman as "a dark romantic man with curly black hair" (Meyers 116).

Meyers also stood out among Fitzgerald biographers for having no reservations whatever about the relationship between Zelda and the naval aviator. Where others speculated about what might have happened, Meyers *knew* exactly what happened and refused to pussyfoot around. He also adopted an air of superiority to the principals, exhibiting a bare tolerance for Scott and an alarming lack of sympathy for Zelda. He had no doubts, for example, about what motivated her summer infidelity: "After five years of marriage, [she] feared she had passed the peak of beauty and had to prove she was still attractive to men. She felt her life was empty, resented Scott's successful career, wanted to make him jealous." Hence it was easy for "Jozan, using his French charm . . . [to] invite Zelda to his apartment and seduce her." Then he abandoned her, leaving her suicidal. On the whole, Meyers concluded, this was a misfortune for Fitzgerald as a writer. "If Zelda had left him for Jozan in 1924,

Scott would have had another lost love to inspire his work and been spared the horrors of her insanity in the 1930s" (Meyers 116-17).

THE SHOWDOWN

Arriving at the correct name and hair color of the French aviator who courted Zelda hardly ranks in importance as compared to what the Fitzgeralds *did* about the affair. Here, too, the reports of the various biographers vary widely.

Almost all of the chroniclers noted that Scott was used to men falling in love with Zelda and that generally it pleased him, though in this case matters got out of hand. Turnbull, however, was the first to assert that as a consequence Scott "forced a showdown and delivered an ultimatum which banished Josanne from their lives" (Turnbull 146). This is vaguely worded—what sort of showdown? what was the ultimatum?—and given no documentation whatever.

Milford took up the issue in far greater detail, attributing her account to Scott's conversation with "a relative" years after the event. The relative was quite likely Scottie Fitzgerald, who after initially cooperating with Milford came to dislike her book as unfairly prejudiced against her father. According to this story, Zelda came to Scott in July, told him she loved Jozan, and asked for a divorce. Furious, Scott insisted upon a showdown among the three of them. Jozan would have to face him in Zelda's presence "and ask for her himself," he insisted. The confrontation Scott asked for never took place, although he invented such love-triangle scenes in both *The Great Gatsby* and *Tender Is the Night*.

Milford added that in a burst of anger, Scott locked Zelda in her rooms at the villa, and that she "apparently accepted [his] ultimatum passively and the subject of divorce was dropped" (Milford 112). Milford further linked the end of the affair to Zelda's apparent suicide attempt in August. According to Calvin Tomkins, biographer of Gerald and Sara Murphy in *Living Well Is the Best Revenge* (1971), about three or four in the morning an ashen and trembling Scott Fitzgerald knocked on their door at the Hôtel du Cap in Antibes with the news that Zelda had taken an overdose of sleeping pills. Sara walked her up and down much of the night to keep her from slipping into the long sleep of oblivion (Tomkins 209).

In her biography Mayfield dismissed the sleeping-pill episode as nonsense. Not only was Zelda's story (to Hadley Hemingway) that a young

French flyer had committed suicide after their tragic romance "an absurd invention," but "almost equally incredible [was the Tomkins-Milford] story of Scott's going from St. Raphaël to . . . Antibes—a distance of fifty-two kilometers—at three or four o'clock in the morning, to get help from the Murphys, because Zelda had taken an overdose of sleeping pills" (Mayfield 97). Here Mayfield was happily debunking the assertions of a previous biographer, and one whose book had more or less stolen her thunder. Still, she may well have been right: there is no mention of such a suicide attempt during August 1924 in Scott's *Ledger*.

Mayfield also expanded on the attractiveness of Admiral Jozan, emphasizing that she found him—during an interview no previous biographer had managed to arrange—"unusually charming and handsome." Mayfield described Jozan as "a born leader . . . healthy, athletic, and vigorous, assured": in fact, blessed with "all the qualities Scott would have liked to have." So when Scott became "violently and irrationally jealous" and threatened to "wring the aviator's neck" in a physical struggle (this development mentioned for the first time), Jozan, as the younger and stronger man, judiciously refused to beat him up. Further—another new twist in the story—Mayfield added that when Scott announced he would leave Zelda if she saw Jozan again, the Frenchman asked for and received a transfer to another station (Mayfield 96, Grenberg 8).

In the last of her three books about F. Scott Fitzgerald and their relationship in Hollywood, Sheilah Graham revealed a grandiose angle on the showdown relayed to her by Scott himself. According to Graham's *The Real F. Scott Fitzgerald* (1976), Fitzgerald told her that initially he liked "Jozanne" (yet another misspelling) and was glad he "was willing to pass the hours with Zelda," leaving him free to write. When the frolicking on the beach led to an affair, however, he was so furious that he bought a pistol and challenged Jozan to a duel, in which each man fired a shot without harming the other. "While he was telling me this," Graham remarked, she had the feeling that "the whole episode" had been invented to provide material for a book—as indeed it had, in the McKisco-Barban duel of *Tender Is the Night*. "Did the Fitzgeralds ever do anything just for the sake of doing it, and not to bolster the legend they had created about themselves or to provide Scott with [material] for his fiction?" she asked, with evident exasperation (Graham 61-62).

A minor refinement of the tale emerged in Matthew J. Bruccoli's *Some Sort of Epic Grandeur* (1981). At more than six hundred pages (including apparatus), Bruccoli's was the longest of the Fitzgerald biographies and contained the most factual material. However, inasmuch as he was primarily interested in Fitzgerald as a professional writer, and in his life only in so far as it had an impact on his career, Bruccoli devoted only a page and a half to Zelda and Jozan's summer romance. He accepted Hadley Hemingway's judgment that "the Fitzgeralds developed the Jozan affair into what was virtually a routine they performed, separately and jointly, for their friends." The new piece of information—and like all biographers, Bruccoli was inclined to attach undue significance to anything fresh he could add to the record—came from a letter Fitzgerald wrote to Dr. Robert S. Carroll, Zelda's doctor at Highland Hospital in Asheville, a document Bruccoli unearthed from a Sotheby Parke-Bernet catalogue. Therein Scott falsely claimed to have been a boxer in his youth, when, he says, he sparred with the champion professionals "Tommy and Mike Gibbons." He would have "annialated" [sic] Jozan in two minutes had the aviator been willing to fight him, he maintained (Bruccoli 199-200, 408).

SOURCES AND INTERPRETATION

Reading through the biographies of Scott and Zelda Fitzgerald, one is struck by how much the story—and its interpretation—changes over time. As the evidence accumulates, with each biographer adding whatever he or she has discovered to the mix, the summer romance takes on greater resonance. In the end, examining a relationship that started and stopped in 1924 in books published from 1951 to 2004 makes it almost indisputable that whatever happened four score and some years ago in the south of France really *mattered* to the Fitzgeralds, their marriage, and their careers.

First, let us consider who contributed what to the growing fund of information. Mizener quotes from Zelda's *Save Me the Waltz*, from Scott's *Ledger* and *Notebooks*, and from a letter of his to Max Perkins. From *Save Me the Waltz*, he derives not only the previously cited passage about Jozan's physicality but also Zelda's (or her heroine Alabama's) semi-embittered, semi-resigned reaction to the end of the affair. Jozan went away, leaving her a long letter and a photograph of himself. The photo was "the most beautiful thing she'd ever owned," but she didn't see any point in keeping it. Whatever she'd wanted from him left when he did. "You took what you wanted from life, if you could get it, and you did without the rest." In a footnote Mizener calls Zelda's account of the romance "the most reliable," adding without further explanation that Scott "used his feelings about it" in depicting the relationship between Nicole Diver and Tommy Barban in *Tender Is the Night* and in the story "Image on the Heart," published in the April 1936 *McCall's.*

Mizener's most important find in the *Notebooks* was Fitzgerald's retrospective comment: "That September 1924 I knew something had happened that could never be repaired." From the *Ledger*, presumably written contemporaneously with events like a journal or a diary, Mizener referred to only two entries and compressed them to fit into the flow of his own prose: "A month after the crisis [Scott] noted that they were 'close together' again and in September that the 'trouble [was] clearing away.'" In the letter to his editor Maxwell Perkins dated 27 August, Fitzgerald suggests (without mentioning the affair) that he has matured as a result of the emotional crisis. "It's been a fair summer. I've been unhappy but my work hasn't suffered from it. I am grown at last" (Mizener 178-80).

Turnbull added "How to Live on Practically Nothing a Year" to the source material, with its rhapsodic evocation of the setting: "the liquid dark" as night descends, "the heavy roses and the nightingales in the pines." From *Save Me the Waltz* he took the comment that Edouard somewhat resembled Scott. Jozan "was handsome—in feature not unlike Scott," but he was, in Zelda's phrase, "full of the sun" while Scott was "a moon person": like two sides of the same coin. From the same source Turnbull introduced the detail that the aviator zoomed his plane "perilously low over the Villa Marie" (Turnbull 145).

Milford, the most extensive and conscientious researcher where anything pertaining to Zelda Fitzgerald was concerned, linked Jozan's stunting his airplane dangerously close to the villa's red-tiled roof to similar gestures of homage young American pilots had paid Zelda in Montgomery in 1918. Milford's single greatest coup, though, was locating Jozan and eliciting from him an extensive written account of his summer with the Fitzgeralds. They struck him as "brimming over with life" and so sophisticated that they "brought into our little provincial circle brilliance, imagination and familiarity with a Parisian and international world to which we had no access." Jozan thought of Scott as an "intellectualist," while he described Zelda as eager to take from life every chance it offered (Milford 108-9). The Frenchman acknowledged that he flirted with her and admired her, but matters went no further. This may or may not have been Gallic gallantry.

Judging from *Save Me the Waltz*, Zelda was extremely attracted to the handsome young French pilot. In this passage, Zelda/Alabama vividly evokes the erotic power of Edouard Jozan. "He drew her body against him till she felt the blades of his bones carving her own," Alabama Knight recalls. "He was bronze and smelled of the sand and sun: she felt him naked underneath the starched linen. She didn't think of [her husband] David. She hoped he hadn't seen; she didn't care. She felt as if she would like to be kissing Jacques Chevre-Feuille on the top of the Arc de Triomphe" (qtd. in Milford 109-10). In his Goncourt Prize–winning 2007 novel *Alabama Song*, as yet untranslated into English, Gilles Simon portrays his fictional Zelda as carried away by Jozan's physical appeal.

Milford's citation of this "explicitly sensual" prose—as highly charged sexually as anything in Scott's work—is but one example of her intelligent use of sources. After consulting Scott's *Ledger*, for instance, she usefully provides the exact language of Scott's four monthly entries in 1924 about the affair. July: "The Big Crisis—13th of July"; August: "Zelda and I close together"; September: "Trouble clearing away"; October: "Last sight of Josanne" (Milford 111-12).

These telescopic comments barely scratch the surface of what went on in Valescure. For further information, Milford interviewed not only Hadley Hemingway but also Sara and Gerald Murphy and Gilbert Seldes. The Murphys, who knew Scott and Zelda well and saw a good deal of them in the summer of 1924, apparently assumed that the affair—like so many among their Riviera friends—had become adulterous. "Jozan wasn't someone for her to talk to," Sara said. "I must say everyone knew about it but Scott." Yet Seldes recalled that when he and his new bride visited the Fitzgeralds early in August, a few weeks after the "Big Crisis," they detected "not a hint of discord" between Scott and Zelda (Milford 110).

Given access to psychiatric records by Scottie Fitzgerald (records that have subsequently remained closed to biographers), Milford was able to quote extensively from an "autobiography" that Zelda wrote for Dr. Oscar Forel following her breakdown in 1930. In that document, Zelda cited two great emotional events of her life. First, "[m]y marriage, after which I was in another world, one for which I was not qualified or prepared, because of my inadequate education." Next, "[a] love affair with a French aviator in St. Raphael. I was locked in my villa for one month to prevent me from seeing him. This lasted for five years. When I knew my husband had another woman in California I was upset because the life over there appeared to me so superficial, but finally I was not hurt because I knew I had done the same thing when I was younger" (qtd. in Milford 174-75). As an avenue of escape, Zelda wrote, she immersed herself in the ballet.

The "locked in her villa" item may well have been a fabrication, like Zelda's elaborate sorrow over the tragic "suicide" of her lover. If she was so sequestered, no one else seems to have noticed. And this particular detail seems to trace back to Scott and Zelda's correspondence in 1919. At that time, even though they were engaged, she regularly wrote him provocative letters about her dates with other young men. These so disturbed Scott that he repeatedly proposed she ought to be locked up "like the princess in her tower."

Milford was also able to draw upon correspondence back and forth between the Fitzgeralds in 1932, after Zelda wrote *Save Me the Waltz* and sent it, without telling her husband, to Max Perkins, as well as Scott's letter to Dr. Mildred Squires at the Phipps Clinic in Baltimore, where Zelda was then confined. In that communication Fitzgerald stressed the lasting significance of his wife's summer romance: "Her affair with Eduard Josanne in 1925 and mine with [actress] Lois Moran in 1927 [in Hollywood], which was a sort of revenge shook something out of us, but we can't both go on paying and paying forever. And yet I feel that's the whole trouble back of all this."

By "all this" Scott presumably meant their then tortured marriage, the trouble compounded by Zelda's mental illness and his own excessive drinking. In a revealing remark, he traced a symbiotic connection between her psychological disturbance and his addiction to alcohol: "Liquor on my mouth is sweet to her; I cherish her most extravagant hallucinations" (Milford 222). They were in it together, coveting each other's weaknesses.

Sara Mayfield, whose book closely followed Milford's, only slightly expanded on her predecessor's fund of information. From *Save Me the Waltz*, she noted that Jacques's fictional family name, Chevre-Feuille, meant "honeysuckle" in French. Interviewing Jozan face-to-face, she found him still charming at seventy years of age. Furthermore, Mayfield visited Scott and Zelda at Juan-les-Pins in the summer of 1926, and as an Alabama girl herself understood the ways of the Southern coquette. In her confident assurance that Zelda's affair amounted to nothing more than an innocent summer entertainment, Mayfield stands at the opposite pole from Jeffrey Meyers, who took the liberty of following Zelda into Jozan's apartment to witness her infidelity.

André LeVot, in his 1983 biography, made the most significant advance toward untangling the affair since the discoveries of Milford thirteen years earlier. Working from resources unavailable to or neglected by earlier writers, LeVot began to plumb the psychological depths. The first of these resources was Zelda Fitzgerald's unfinished novel "Caesar's Things," which she worked on during the last six years of her life. In that novel, she returned obsessively to the affair that had been central to *Save Me the Waltz*. The basic situation is much the same in both novels. The heroine is married to an artist who is committed to his work. She meets a young Frenchman who bears a certain similarity to her husband, but "whose work is not a rival to her and who is free to give her as much as she longs to receive." In "Caesar's Things," however, the given names are changed to emphasize the emotional interconnections between all points of the triangle. The woman is Janno, her husband Jacob, the lover Jacques.

The real reason Janno embarked on the affair, LeVot commented, was to "break out of the purgatory in which Jacob has confined her." Her husband invests all of his vitality in his painting, while she merely sits and waits, feeling dispossessed and withering away. Even when Jacob puts an end to the affair, he postpones dealing with the problem in order to complete his work in progress. "I'll get out of here as soon as I can," he says. "In the mean-time you are not to leave these premises. You understand?" Janno understood, all right. She "told her husband that she loved the French officer and her husband locked her up in the villa": again the locked door, a detail in her autobiography for Dr. Forel (1930) that had gone unused in *Save Me the Waltz* (1932).

LeVot went back to Fitzgerald's *Notebooks* for still more important insights. In the same section of the notes that mentions something having happened in the summer of 1924 "that never could be repaired," LeVot found two other comments that refer to the affair. In one of these Scott expresses compassion for Zelda's plight: "He was sorry, knowing how she would pay." The other suggests that Scott himself had been complicit in allowing or even arranging for his wife's dereliction. It reads, "Feeling of proxy in passion; strange encouragement." Something of what Scott apparently meant by "encouragement" was to emerge in "Caesar's Things." When Janno and Jacob first encounter Jacques, Janno is reluctant to approach him. Jacob insists that she do so.

Altogether LeVot establishes himself as a sensitive interpreter of the incident, with an apparent understanding of love affairs. When Zelda exercises her flirtatious charm, for example, LeVot observes that she "did it so outrageously . . . that the very exuberance she brought to it absolved her of any guilty intent." Flirting *that* openly, he suggests, could be an excellent way of warding off suspicion (LeVot 174-77).

Relatively little new intelligence about the affair is advanced in my biography and those of James Mellow and Jeffrey Meyers. In *Fool for Love: F. Scott Fitzgerald* (1983), I discuss the way that Fitzgerald's story "Image on the Heart" parallels the events on the Riviera more than a decade earlier. In that story, the male protagonist, who has just married a younger woman, discovers that she had spent the day before their wedding with a French aviator. Although she maintains that nothing happened during that time, she offers her husband an annulment. He declines the offer, deciding to let her indiscretion pass. They ride away on their honeymoon, the husband silently thinking "that he would never know" the truth and worried that the question might "haunt their marriage like a ghost" (SD 70-71). As J. Gerald Kennedy points out in his essay on "Fitzgerald's Expatriate Years," both this story and the account of the French mercenary Tommy Barban winning Nicole Diver away from her husband in *Tender Is the Night* the previous year strongly suggest that Zelda's luminous portrayal of Jacques Chevre-Feuille in *Save Me the Waltz* aroused Scott's "retrospective jealousy" (Kennedy 139-40).

Zelda was acutely aware that this kind of uncertainty might trouble her husband. In her interview with Henry Dan Piper in 1947 that I introduced into the record, Zelda said she "regretted having flirted with so many men and never telling Scott how far she'd gone with them, letting him guess the worst" (qtd. in SD 71). Inasmuch as Zelda had become his lover in advance of their wedding, Scott was forever dubious about her virtue. As Hemingway mentions in *A Moveable Feast*, when Fitzgerald asked him at their first meeting whether he had slept with Hadley before they were married, Hemingway wasn't of much help. "I don't know," he said. "I can't remember" (EH 127).

Like LeVot, Mellow emphasizes the psychological importance of Scott's "feeling proxy in passion" note. Mellow also wonders whether the fact that neither Scott nor Zelda ever spelled Jozan's name correctly might be construed as evidence of her marital fidelity, even though a letter she wrote Scott in 1930 (cited for the first time by Mellow) would seem to argue otherwise. "Then there was Josen," Zelda's letter admits, "and you were justifiably angry." In addition, Mellow notes that René and Bobbé, as portrayed in *Save Me the Waltz*, were in all likelihood gay. The two of them, in Zelda's description, "protruded insistently from their white beach clothes and talked in undertones of Arthur Rimbaud" (Mellow 210-14; Cline 148).

It may well be that after Milford (especially) and LeVot, there was not much left for latter-day biographers to find out about the affair. But there was still room in which to venture new interpretations. In three twenty-first-century books, Kendall Taylor, Sally Cline, and Linda Wagner-Martin all attempt to understand what the affair of the summer of 1924 meant to the relationship between the Fitzgeralds—with particular emphasis on Zelda's subsequent position.

Taylor uncovered but one new scrap of evidence in *Sometimes Madness Is Wisdom* (2001): Zelda's card of entry, dated 10 June 1924, to the Salon Privé of the Monte Carlo Casino. For Taylor, this served as evidence that Zelda and Jozan visited the casino together on that date. Taylor also assumed that Zelda slept with the Frenchman. "When attracted," she wrote, "Zelda was sexually aggressive and Jozan had ample opportunities to respond."

In assessing the effects of the affair, Taylor invades Zelda's consciousness—a biographical leap based primarily on Zelda's observations in her 1930 autobiography for Dr. Forel. Whatever may have happened during the summer romance, Taylor observed, the incident "generated a deep distrust and left an indelible scar. When locked in the Villa Marie, Zelda realized she was also locked into her marriage and . . . determined to have no further romantic liaisons. Deeply troubled that she might never again be happy with Fitzgerald, yet aware of her inability to survive on her own, she recognized a power shift in their relationship and the reality struck her painfully" (Taylor 138-40).

Cline's *Zelda Fitzgerald: Her Voice in Paradise* (2002) went further in postulating that the summer romance transformed the marriage, placing Scott firmly in control. Cline quoted more extensively from "Caesar's Things" than any previous commentator. In this unfinished work, her second fictional revisiting of the affair, Zelda described at least three occasions when her heroine, Janno, kissed Jacques long and with undue enthusiasm. In fact, Janno reflects, she should never have kissed him at all. "First she should never have kissed Jacques; then she shouldn't have kissed her husband; then after the kissing had become spiritual vivisection and half-masochistic there should not have been any more." Cline cited another section of "Caesar's Things" to provide a gloss on Janno's tortured feelings. "He that looketh on a woman to lust after hath committed adultery with her in his heart already," she quotes from the Bible, and then reflects that "adultery was adultery and it would have been impossible for her to love two men at once, to give herself to simultaneous intimacies."

Although "*no* concrete evidence" exists that Zelda slept with Jozan, Cline wrote, "for the morbidly jealous Scott, who still had mixed-up Irish Catholic monogamous feelings for Zelda, the fact that she was entertaining a *desire* to commit adultery would be almost as much a sin as actually committing adultery." In the aftermath, Cline concluded, Scott appropriated the affair to establish his position as the controlling partner in the Fitzgeralds' marriage: "The reason why Scott fictionalized and heightened the romance to include these fabrications [e.g., the confrontation, fight, or duel between himself and Jozan] was that he was then able to share it, thus once more taking over an important piece of Zelda's life. That she allowed him to do so illustrates her emotional dependency upon him." To back up these statements, Cline reverted once more to "Caesar's Things." Once the affair was ended, "Janno grew indomitably loyal and devoted to Jacob. . . . Jacob was somehow the center of the whole business" (Cline 150-54).

Linda Wagner-Martin's *Zelda Sayre Fitzgerald: An American Woman's Life* (2004) arrived at a psychological reading of the affair and its aftereffects that, like Cline's, placed Scott in a position of dominance. Feeling certain that Zelda did indeed attempt to kill herself in late August 1924, Wagner-Martin imagined how it must have been for Zelda once Jozan was banished from her life. Still "beautiful and vivacious" at twenty-four, but "with an increasing sense of her inferiority," Zelda suffered in two different ways: "from the loss of what she assumed to be the great love of her life" and also from her own sense of help-lessness. "More than ever," Wagner-Martin observed, "she saw that she was in the control of her husband: Scott had the money, he had the power, he had the reputation. What would she do if she tried to leave him? How would she and Scottie live? And would she be emotionally strong enough to make a break?"

In Wagner-Martin's view, Zelda was so beset with these worries that she adopted a posture of submissiveness, ceding all authority to her husband. (That might explain why Gilbert Seldes and his wife, on their early August visit, observed only serenity between the Fitzgeralds.) Once the affair was over and Scott asserted his control, Zelda spent more time with Scottie and helped Scott with his revisions of *The Great Gatsby*. At least for a time, she submerged her yearnings for an identity of her own and became a virtual Stepford wife. Then, Wagner-Martin proposed, the Fitzgeralds' marriage descended into sadomasochism.

In support of this interpretation, she cited a November 1924 letter from Zelda to Scott, accusing him of "bestial behavior during love-making." Although this brought on a severe asthma attack, Zelda did not threaten to leave Scott. In effect Zelda accepted the sadomasochistic pattern of their marriage, assuming "the position of the masochist." But the longer they played these separate roles, Wagner-Martin suggested, the closer they came to "rational violence" and mental breakdown.

Wagner-Martin contributed an important fragment to the tale, drawn from the embittered confrontation between Zelda and Scott on the afternoon of 28 May 1933. With Dr. Thomas Rennie and a stenographer in attendance, the Fitzgeralds tried to talk out their problems on that day. In the 114-page account of this session, Scott repeatedly insisted that as the professional writer in the family, he should have sole access to whatever happened to either one of them for his fiction. According to his lights, Zelda had appropriated *his* material in *Save Me the Waltz*, and now she was threatening to take even more by writing about her illness. He went so far as to say, and say again, that Zelda had tried to destroy him by falling in love with Jozan while he was "doing the best work of [his] life" on *The Great Gatsby*. (Bruccoli, who printed a portion of the 28 May transcript in *Some Sort of Epic Grandeur*, did not include this detail.) "As far as destroying you is concerned," Zelda responded, "I have considered you first in everything I have tried to do in my life" (Wagner-Martin 84-88, 168).

At bottom the conversation between the Fitzgeralds that May afternoon in 1933 boiled down to the issue of who was in charge of their relationship. Zelda wanted to be free of her husband's criticism and control and to do her own writing. Scott wanted—and expected—her to be dutiful to him, as the breadwinner in the family. She criticized him for his persistent drinking and occasional cruelty. He disparaged her as an artist and a psychological cripple. It made for an ugly show of a marriage gone wrong—a marriage that may well have been beyond recovery after the summer of 1924, when something happened that could not be repaired, something they had to pay for during the rest of their lives.

AFTERWORD

This study of Zelda Fitzgerald's affair with Edouard Jozan is based on fourteen biographical treatments of the subject written over more than half a century. Almost all of these contribute pieces of evidence into the record, and a few of them cite documents that are crucial to arriving at the facts of the matter. It is a cumulative process, with latter-day biographers standing on the shoulders of their predecessors as they survey the ground.

Obviously, you need the *facts* first, and then you proceed toward some version of the *truth*, in full awareness that the entire truth will, in all its complications, remain finally inaccessible. The process resembles the search for what Hemingway called the "true gen" in warfare, the phrase suggesting an analogy between the digging of the biographer and the work of G2, or military intelligence, in trying to make sense of reconnaissance photographs and prisoner interviews and intercepted communications. The biographer might also be compared to a forensic detective assigned to find whether a crime has been perpetrated, and if so, by whom and to whom, as well as when and where and—most difficult of all to ascertain—why. The elusive issue of people's motivations, motivations that those involved may well have been unable to understand themselves, forces the biographer into the role of an amateur psychologist. Manifestly, few humans are capable of doing all of these jobs thoroughly and well. It can safely be said that the single trait all biographers share is a certain arrogance as they undertake to understand how it must have been, say, for Zelda and Scott and Edouard a long time ago.

The literary biographer, at least, has the benefit of access to the writings of her or his subjects. In fact, the most persuasive testimony that the affair was adulterous and not an insignificant summer flirtation comes from Zelda and Scott themselves. Both of them made serious fictional capital out of the romance, and more than once. This strongly suggests that the affair meant far more to them than mere source material for a performance with which to entertain their friends.

Still, the wide disparity between the judgments of the Fitzgeralds' various biographers testifies to the precarious nature of the craft. A few felt certain that Zelda was unfaithful to Scott with Jozan; others were sure that she was not. Some chroniclers thought the affair of little importance; others saw it as of great significance. From fourteen books you get fourteen different accounts—a scornful treatment, a bare recital of the facts, a modestly speculative approach, a fiercely authoritative one, several psychological readings, and so on. This illustrates what has often been remarked: that every biography conceals within itself the autobiography of its author. No matter how devoutly they embrace objectivity as their goal, biographers' personalities and opinions and biases emerge as they tell their separate stories.

Let my own case serve as an example. In writing *Fool for Love*, I emphasized an angle that others tended to ignore: the way in which *not knowing* what his wife had done exacerbated Fitzgerald's feelings of jealousy. It is true that taking this approach enabled me to introduce both "Image on the Heart," Scott's 1935 story, and Henry Dan Piper's interview with Zelda into the record. Still, you might well conclude that at least as much as F. Scott Fitzgerald, I was somewhat troubled by epistemological uncertainties in these our lives and shared his tendency to harbor and cultivate jealousy. You might even be right.

THE BIOGRAPHICAL TREATMENT (IN ORDER OF PUBLICATION)

Mizener, Arthur. *The Far Side of Paradise: A Biography of F. Scott Fitzgerald.* Boston: Houghton Mifflin, 1951.

Turnbull, Andrew. *Scott Fitzgerald.* New York: Scribner, 1962.

Hemingway, Ernest. *A Moveable Feast.* New York: Scribner, 1964.

Milford, Nancy. *Zelda: A Biography.* New York: Harper and Row, 1970.

Mayfield, Sara. *Exiles from Paradise: Zelda and Scott Fitzgerald.* New York: Delacorte, 1971.

Graham, Sheilah. *The Real F. Scott Fitzgerald: Thirty-Five Years Later.* New York: Grosset and Dunlap, 1976.

Bruccoli, Matthew J. *Some Sort of Epic Grandeur: The Life of F. Scott Fitzgerald.* New York: Harcourt Brace Jovanovich, 1981.

LeVot, André. *F. Scott Fitzgerald: A Biography.* New York: Doubleday, 1983.

Donaldson, Scott. *Fool for Love: F. Scott Fitzgerald.* New York: Congdon and Weed, 1983.

Mellow, James. *Invented Lives: F. Scott and Zelda Fitzgerald.* Boston: Houghton Mifflin, 1984.

Meyers, Jeffrey. *Scott Fitzgerald: A Biography.* New York: HarperCollins, 1993.

Taylor, Kendall. *Sometimes Madness Is Wisdom: Zelda and Scott Fitzgerald; A Marriage.* New York: Ballantine, 2001.

Cline, Sally. *Zelda Fitzgerald: Her Voice in Paradise.* New York: Arcade, 2003.

Wagner-Martin, Linda. *Zelda Sayre Fitzgerald: An American Woman's Life.* New York: Palgrave Macmillan, 2004.

ADDITIONAL SOURCES

Fitzgerald, F. Scott. *F. Scott Fitzgerald: A Life in Letters.* Edited by Matthew J. Bruccoli. New York: Simon and Schuster, 1994.

———. *The Great Gatsby.* New York: Modern Library, 1934.

Grenberg, Bruce L. "Fitzgerald's 'Figured Curtain': Personality and History in *Tender Is the Night.*" *Critical Essays on "Tender Is the Night."* Edited by Milton R. Stern. Boston: G. K. Hall, 1986. 211-37.

Kennedy, J. Gerald. "Fitzgerald's Expatriate Years and the European Stories." *The Cambridge Companion to F. Scott Fitzgerald.* Edited by Ruth Prigozy. Cambridge: Cambridge University Press, 2002. 118-42.

Tomkins, Calvin. *Living Well Is the Best Revenge.* New York: Viking Press, 1971.

FOUR

Scott and Dottie

In November 2013 I was among those who received an e-mail from the Fitzgerald scholar Jackson Bryer. He was reading for accuracy the manuscript of Maureen Corrigan's *So We Read On: How "The Great Gatsby" Came to Be and Why It Endures* (2014) and had a number of questions to ask. One query involved a possible romantic relationship between F. Scott Fitzgerald (1896–1940) and Dorothy Parker (1893–1967). In Corrigan's manuscript, Bryer pointed out, a "claim is made that Fitzgerald was 'briefly' Dorothy Parker's 'lover.' Is this based on any firm evidence?"

At the time I was putting the final touches on *The Impossible Craft: Literary Biography* (2015), my book about the abundant difficulties of arriving at the truth about the lives of writers—"licensed liars," Victoria Glendinning calls them, people who by occupation invent fictions, and not only about others. I immediately repaired to my bookcase, trying to discover whether the Fitzgerald-Parker relationship had reached a climax and what various biographers had written about the rumored affair.

The two most thorough biographies, Matthew J. Bruccoli's *Some Sort of Epic Grandeur: The Life of F. Scott Fitzgerald* (1981) and Nancy Milford's *Zelda: A Biography* (1970), have nothing to say about any romance between Scott Fitzgerald and Dorothy Parker. Neither do the three earliest Fitzgerald biographies: Arthur Mizener's *The Far Side of Paradise: A Biography of F. Scott Fitzgerald* (1951), Andrew Turnbull's *Scott Fitzgerald* (1959), and Henry Dan Piper's *F. Scott Fitzgerald: A Critical Portrait* (1965). Her name appears only twice in Mizener, once in Piper, and not at all in Turnbull. A number of books I checked, however, mention it as if it were a fact that the two writers engaged in a brief affair. These include my own *Fool for Love: F. Scott Fitzgerald* (1983), André LeVot's *F. Scott Fitzgerald: A Biography* (1983), James R. Mellow's *Invented Lives: F. Scott and Zelda Fitzgerald* (1984), and Jeffrey Meyers's *Scott Fitzgerald: A Biography* (1994).

Upon further examination it became clear that there was a single source behind all of these assertions: Lillian Hellman's autobiographical *An Unfinished Woman: A Memoir* (1969), wherein on page 57 Hellman reports that at a Hollywood party on the evening of 12 July 1937 Parker told her that she had slept with Scott Fitzgerald "in a one or two night affair"—wouldn't she remember which?—some years previously. Obviously this rather vague statement was unavailable to Mizener, Turnbull, and Piper, who wrote their biographies before *An Unfinished Woman* appeared. In addition, Milford may well have completed her work on *Zelda* in advance of Hellman's memoir. Bruccoli, who surely knew about Hellman's book, chose to ignore it, either because he regarded it as unimportant to the literary career of Fitzgerald or because he suspected that much of what Hellman wrote was not to be trusted. There is no question that Hellman invented stories and altered facts in *An Unfinished Woman* and that her account of what happened on 12 July 1937 is extremely unreliable. Yet there's no particular reason why she might have made up the conversation with Parker about her fling with Fitzgerald. Marion Meade, whose *Dorothy Parker: What Fresh Hell Is This?* (1989) stands as the authoritative biography, apparently accepted Hellman's account as accurate but of minimal importance.

Whether they were lovers or not, Fitzgerald and Parker were demonstrably friends who spent time together in New York and Hollywood, on the Riviera and in the Swiss Alps, at various times between 1919 and 1940. This twenty-year relationship between major twentieth-century American writers has been largely neglected by biographers and critics. This seems to me unfortunate, partly because of the similarities in the lives and careers of Parker and Fitzgerald. They were both alcoholics, subject to depression. They shared a number of close friends, Gerald and Sara Murphy among them. As writers they both began with a fascination with the theatre. As their fiction matured, they both made literary capital out of the dirty little secret in American culture that social class matters, even—or especially—in a society that denies that it does. Despite earning substantial sums from their writing, they both struggled financially, spending more than they could afford and depending on inflated Hollywood salaries to make ends meet. They both turned sharply left in their politics during the 1930s.

1919–1924: NEW YORK AND ENVIRONS

According to Meade, Dorothy Parker first met Scott Fitzgerald in 1919, when he was working for an advertising agency in New York, and Parker, unhappily married, was turning out clever light verse and savage reviews as the drama critic for *Vanity Fair*. At the time, Meade wrote, Fitzgerald told Parker about his plans to marry Zelda Sayre, "'the most beautiful girl in Alabama and Georgia,' even though he was in the midst of a torrid liaison with an English actress"—a liaison that has so far escaped the attention of all Fitzgerald biographers.

A year later Scott and Zelda came back to New York to be married—Fitzgerald now the acclaimed author of *This Side of Paradise*—and to embark on their project of shocking the bourgeoisie through wild and well-publicized partying. Parker's first sight of the couple in 1920 was of Zelda riding on the hood of a taxicab with Scott on the roof. They looked "as though they had just stepped out of the sun," she observed. "Their youth was striking," and "everyone wanted to meet him." Parker had reservations about Zelda, however: "I never thought she was beautiful. She was very blonde with a candy box face and little bow mouth, very much on a small scale" (Parker herself was 4'11" and slightly built), "and there was something petulant about her."

Despite the success of his novel, Fitzgerald was often broke. In the fall he asked Parker to lend him one hundred dollars, and apparently she did. An entry for October 1920 in Fitzgerald's *Ledger*—a valuable source for mentions of people whose lives intersected with his—notes that "Zelda hides $100 from Dorothy Parker."

By that time Parker had become a celebrity in New York literary circles, known for her biting wit. Together with other journalists and playwrights, among them Parker's great friends Robert Benchley, Alexander Woollcott, and George S. Kaufman, she was a charter member of the Algonquin Round Table—"The Gonk," they called it—where at weekly lunches they traded banter and barbs. Parker was a star among stars in the group. Here are a few samples drawn from the 2006 edition of *The Portable Dorothy Parker* and

Meade's biography. Challenged to use horticulture in a sentence: "you can lead a whore to culture but you can't make her think." Modifying a cliché: "Brevity is the soul of lingerie." Reviewing a novel: "Theodore Dreiser / Should ought to write nicer." A favorite theme in her poems, offering cynical commentary on the serial love affairs that periodically brightened and darkened her days:

> Lady, lady, should you meet
> One whose ways are all discreet,
> One who murmurs that his wife
> Is the lodestar of his life,
> One who keeps assuring you
> That he never was untrue,
> Never loved another one . . .
> Lady, lady, better run!

And:

> By the time you swear you're his,
> Shivering and sighing,
> And he vows his passion is
> Infinite, undying—
> Lady, make a note of this:
> One of you is lying.

And of course the famous couplet she regretted having composed, since it was so often used as a commonplace summarizing her work: "Men seldom make passes / At girls who wear glasses."

In her play reviews, she described Katharine Hepburn's performance as "run[ning] the gamut of emotions from A to B," recommended a show as an excellent opportunity to do some knitting—or, "if you don't knit, bring a book"—and refused to print the names of another show's author or cast, for she was "not going to tell on them." Her reviews were so consistently devastating that in January 1920 she was fired by *Vanity Fair*, an event that inspired her colleagues Robert Benchley and Robert Sherwood to resign from the magazine in protest. These developments, duly reported in the *New York Times*, worked out well for all three of them (as well as for Fitzgerald's Princeton friend Edmund Wilson, who replaced Benchley as managing editor). Parker continued to publish her light verse in *Life* and the *Saturday Evening Post*, and she began a series of short prose sketches for the *Ladies' Home Journal* that skewered the pretensions of (mostly) women in a Tuesday club, at a dinner party, in an apartment house, and at a summer hotel.

Parker, who had been brought up in and around New York, was the youngest child of Eliza and J. Henry Rothschild—though not, as she pointed out, one of "those Rothschilds." Her mother died when she was three, and her father, a success in the garment industry, died in 1913, when she was twenty. The next year she sold her first poem for money (twelve dollars) and began her long career as a professional writer. Although she'd dropped out of school at fourteen, Parker brought a keen eye and an excellent command of language to her work. She was at her best in dialogue and monologue that effectively characterized the speaker(s), and she consistently regarded her characters, including herself, with a sharply satiric bent: "They say of me, and well they should, / It's doubtful if I come to good."

She was married in 1917 to Edwin Pond Parker II ("Eddie") of Hartford, Connecticut, an engaging young man in the brokerage business who soon became an addict, first to drugs, then to drink. The marriage foundered, leading Parker to serial affairs, including a disastrous one with the newspaperman Charles MacArthur that ended in 1922 with an abortion and the first of her several suicide attempts. "Mrs. Parker," as she liked to be called, began drinking heavily during that time, but in its initial stages the alcohol did not affect her appearance or her reputation as the life of the party. Late in life she described herself as "just a little Jewish girl trying to be cute," and cute she certainly was when the Fitzgeralds arrived on the New York scene: a "mischievous little elf," a petite brunette with gorgeous big eyes beneath her bangs. Donald Ogden Stewart thought her "absolutely devastating."

From the beginning Fitzgerald was attracted to Parker, both for her person and her accomplishments, while, according to Edmund Wilson, she was "beglamored by the idea of Scott Fitzgerald" and thought him "attractive and sweet when he wanted to be nice." There is no evidence that this mutual attraction led to any adulterous conduct in the early 1920s, although they liked and respected each other as fellow professionals. In January 1922 Fitzgerald asked Maxwell Perkins to send review copies of *The Beautiful and Damned* to thirty influential reviewers and writers, including Dorothy Parker. In the same year she published a poem called "The Flapper."

All spotlights focus on her pranks.
All tongues her prowess herald.
For which she well may render thanks
To God and Scott Fitzgerald.

They met regularly at literary gatherings in Manhattan and at the raucous Gatsbyesque parties thrown by the newspaperman Herbert Bayard Swope at his home in Great Neck, two miles from the Fitzgeralds' eighteen-month residence there and close to the house of Ring Lardner, a drinking companion and friend to both Fitzgerald and Parker. Celebrities and would-be celebrities from the theater world abounded at these parties, along with "retired debauchees and actresses."

The writers who came to those parties, or most of them, were eager to make their mark in the theater. Both Fitzgerald and Parker suffered painful defeats trying to do so. The failure of his comedy *The Vegetable*, which opened on the road late in 1923 and never made it to Broadway, disappointed Fitzgerald deeply. He'd counted on its success as a source of money and was driven—in the long run, fortunately—to abandon his theatrical dreams, move to France, and devote his energies to a novel that brought the frantic Great Neck scene alive as the site of Jay Gatsby's/Trimalchio's revels.

Parker's play *Close Harmony* suffered a similar fate a year later. The play opened in Wilmington, Delaware, in November and came to Broadway before Christmas. The reviews were excellent, calling attention to the sharply delineated characters and their "uncannily authentic and very funny dialogue." Nonetheless the public stayed home. As Lardner wrote Fitzgerald on 9 January 1925, "Dorothy Parker's 'Close Harmony' got great notices and was, we thought, a dandy play, but it flopped in three weeks."

1926–1930: OVERSEAS

With Fitzgerald decamped to Europe, he and Parker did not see each other until the spring of 1926. Oddly enough it was Ernest Hemingway who facilitated their reunion. Scott and Ernest had met in Paris in April 1925, just after the publication of *The Great Gatsby*, and immediately bonded, with Fitzgerald as the established author advising and encouraging his younger and manifestly talented companion. In February 1926, Hemingway came to New

York to break his contract with Boni and Liveright and sign on with Maxwell Perkins at Scribner for *The Torrents of Spring* and *The Sun Also Rises*—an undertaking in good part orchestrated by Fitzgerald. After switching publishers, Hemingway stayed in the city another week to mingle with the literary crowd, including Parker and Benchley.

Parker was more or less carried away by the extraordinarily handsome Hemingway. The publicity photograph showing him smiling with slanted cap and shirt flung open above a dark sweater made women "want to go right out and get him and bring him home, stuffed." They got along well, sharing a conviction that writing was bloody hard work, with constant revision required to make it come right. And Parker was so fascinated by Hemingway's stories about the expatriate community in Paris that she suddenly decided to go overseas. She and Benchley made the crossing on the same ship with Hemingway and, once in Paris, spent a couple of convivial evenings with the Hemingways and the Fitzgeralds at the Closerie des Lilas. Four years later, with the mentally ill Zelda "gone to the Clinique," Fitzgerald returned to the restaurant alone, "remembering the happy time [he] had had there with Ernest, Hadley, Dorothy Parker & Benchley."

Back in the States, Parker was a regular on the guest list for the inebriated house parties the Fitzgeralds threw at Ellerslie, the estate outside Wilmington, Delaware, that they were renting. A note in Fitzgerald's *Ledger* for March 1928 reads simply "Dorothy Parker" with no elaboration. It was a hard time for her. She was divorced from Eddie Parker on 31 March, and her current romance with John Wiley Garrett II—another of the initialed, tall, Ivy League patrician males she fancied, despite their having very little in common—was not going well. Perhaps Fitzgerald saw her in New York that month. Certainly he did see her in the summer of 1929, on the Riviera, this time in association with Gerald and Sara Murphy.

The Fitzgeralds came overseas early that year and rented a villa in Cannes for the summer. Once a week or so they saw the Murphys, the wealthy, charming, and star-crossed expatriates who went out of their way to befriend a number of artists and writers, including Hemingway, Fitzgerald, Dos Passos, Fernand Leger, and Pablo Picasso. In June 1929 the Murphys invited Dorothy Parker and Benchley, along with his wife and two boys, to visit them at their Villa America in Antibes.

Parker's reputation had taken off that year, propelled by the success of "Big Blonde," her tale of a woebegone party girl that won the O. Henry award for the best story of 1929. Highly autobiographical in its unveiling of Parker's out-of-control drinking, haphazard affairs, and attempt at suicide through Veronal pills, "Big Blonde" ran to twenty-three pages in the *Bookman* for February 1929. That was much longer than her usual story length of two or three or five pages and inspired the Viking Press, a brand-new publishing firm founded by George Oppenheimer and Harold Guinzburg—"the Boys," in Parker's lexicon—to offer her an advance for a novel.

At the Murphys' she was installed at the Bastide, a cottage modernized with plumbing and electricity. Feeling invigorated and cutting back on drink, she quickly sent the *New Yorker* three poems and two short stories, and made some progress on the novel-never-to-be that she proposed to call *Sonnets in Suicide*. Having helped deliver Hemingway to Scribner, Fitzgerald urged Max Perkins in June 1929 to go after Parker as well. She was "at a high point," a valuable literary property, and, he warned Perkins, "I wouldn't lose any time about this if it interests you."

He wished he could have seen more of Parker during that summer, Fitzgerald comments in a 23 August letter to Hemingway, "but we are, thank God, desperately unpopular and not invited anywhere." A few weeks later, in another letter to Hemingway, he spelled out the principal reason for that unpopularity: his own exasperating behavior when in his cups. He was given to insulting others and destroying the crockery, for example. As Zelda recalled of that period, he had "disgraced" himself at Philip and Ellen Barry's party, on a yacht in Monte Carlo, and at the casino with Gerald and Dotty. "A last party with Dotty and Gerald," Fitzgerald cryptically noted in his *Ledger* for September 1929, and, more explicitly, "being drunk and snubbed." He coveted those snubs, making lists of them in his notebooks.

His "latest tendency," he wrote Hemingway, was to collapse into tears around eleven p.m. and tell people he didn't have a friend in the world and didn't much care for anyone else, "including Zelda and often implying current company—after which the current company tend[ed] to become less current and [he woke] up in strange rooms in strange places . . . when drunk I make them all pay and pay."

Among those Fitzgerald managed to alienate was Parker, who, "having been in an equivalent state" of drunken melancholy, lacked patience with his performance. He couldn't really blame her, Fitzgerald said, for "no one likes to see people in moods of despair they themselves have survived." Yet he manifestly resented her having become a favorite at the Villa America.

"The Murphys have given their whole performance for her this summer and I think, tho' she would be the last to admit it, she's had the time of her life."

Within months the Murphys' pleasant and exquisitely organized world began to fall apart when their youngest son, Patrick, contracted tuberculosis. So did the Fitzgeralds' more troubled universe when Zelda, who had become obsessive about her dancing, broke down and was diagnosed as schizophrenic. In hopes of ameliorating Patrick's illness, the Murphys left for Montana-Vermala in the Swiss Alps. There the boy would presumably benefit from the fresh mountain air and dairy-rich diet thought to be best for tubercular patients (there was no known cure at the time). Parker was persuaded to come along, primarily as a companion for Sara Murphy, and stayed through the 1929 Christmas season. Montana-Vermala's Palace Hotel, where Patrick was receiving treatment—really a sanitarium—struck Parker as "jolly no end, no end whatever." The halls were full of doctors in butchers' coats; the rooms were kept so cold that for dinner she wore a tweed suit, a coat over it, a woolen muffler, a knitted cap, and galoshes; and everyone was dying. For Sara's birthday they had a little party with cake and champagne. A nurse and the housekeeper and one of the doctors came, and when Sara's health was drunk to and Gerald kissed her, Parker couldn't stop crying. "Christ, think of all the shits in the world," she wrote Benchley, "and then this happens to the Murphys."

After a visit to New York, where, in lieu of the novel, she put together a collection of stories for Viking, Parker returned to Switzerland in the summer of 1930. By this time the Murphys had taken over a local farmhouse and converted it into a nightclub with a dance band. They called it Harry's Bar. This attempt to lighten the atmosphere largely failed. Patrick's condition remained critical, and the prognosis was not auspicious. In August, Scott Fitzgerald came for a three-day visit, and Parker was "so glad to see him that he misunderstood."

Perhaps Fitzgerald was not "the inevitable male companion" she would choose out of the entire world, she writes in a long letter to Oppenheimer and Guinzburg, but he "was moderately sober, and pretty darn nice." Besides, she couldn't help feeling sorry for him, with Zelda having been institutionalized since January. "Poor kid, he is living in Caux, near Montreux [a setting he was to use to great effect as the scene of Nicole Warren's seduction of Dick Diver in *Tender Is the Night*], and the little girl [Scottie] is in Brittany with a governess, and Zelda is in a sanatorium in Geneva"—an improvement on the "insane asylum" and a hopeful sign that she might "get out some time. Scott hasn't been allowed to see her for months." She knew the Fitzgeralds could be "awful pests," but she couldn't help seeing them as they were ten years earlier, when they first arrived in New York, and Scott had "this crazy success with 'This Side of Paradise,' and they were the golden lad and the golden girl, if ever I saw them. And this is so damn dreary for a conclusion."

1934: NEW YORK

If Scott Fitzgerald and Dorothy Parker did have a brief affair, it probably happened in the spring of 1934, after Zelda's third breakdown. By that time it was becoming clear to her husband, and to her doctors, that she would probably always require institutional care, and Scott would have to look elsewhere for female companionship. In addition, he had finally finished his long slog with *Tender Is the Night*, a serial version of which was running in *Scribner's Magazine* for January, February, March, and April, with official book publication scheduled for 12 April. He felt more or less liberated.

In the previous year Parker had formed a relationship with a young actor named Alan Campbell who had published a few stories in the *New Yorker*. Campbell, eleven years her junior, was usually cast as a juvenile because of his good looks. Marion Meade describes him as resembling a young Scott Fitzgerald before drinking had begun to take its toll. Each of them looked almost too pretty for a man, with fair hair and fine features. Tremendously admiring Parker from the beginning, Campbell took it upon himself to organize her time, manage her money, supervise her diet, shop for her clothes, redo her makeup, redesign her hairstyle, and redecorate her apartment. Most of their friends thought he was gay; perhaps he was bisexual. Certainly they became lovers and moved in together.

That did not mean that Parker would stop seeing other men, though. She and John O'Hara were drinking coffee late one night in October 1933 when she read Fitzgerald's memorial tribute in the *New Republic* to Ring Lardner. Lardner had died at forty-eight, Fitzgerald wrote, after getting less of himself down on paper than any other American writer of the first flight.

> At no time did I feel that I had known him enough, or that anyone knew him—it was not the feeling that there was more stuff in him and that it should come out, it was rather as though, due to some inadequacy

in one's self, one had not penetrated to something unsolved, new and unsaid. That is why one wishes that Ring had written down a larger proportion of what was in his mind and heart. It would have saved him longer for us, and that in itself would be something. But I would like to know what it was, and now I'll go on wishing—what did Ring want, how did he want things to be, how did he think things were?

In these comments Fitzgerald may have been reflecting on his own work as well. How much of himself, his deepest thoughts and fears, had he managed to convey in his fiction? Precious little, perhaps, in his formulaic and lightsome stories for the *Saturday Evening Post*. But surely a great deal in other stories like "Winter Dreams" (1922) and "Babylon Revisited" (1931), and in *The Great Gatsby*, as well as the new novel about Dick Diver that he was at last ready to deliver to Scribner. Parker read the Lardner piece aloud to O'Hara, who kept saying, "Isn't that swell?" "The Gettysburg Address was good too," she replied, and sent a brief note to Fitzgerald: "I think your piece about Ring is the finest and most moving thing I have ever read."

He called to thank her, but they were not to see each other until March 1934, when Zelda was transferred from the Phipps Clinic at Johns Hopkins in Baltimore to Craig House in Beacon, New York, a high-end mental hospital alongside the Hudson River two hours north of the city. Fitzgerald spent most of the next two months in New York, first staying at the Algonquin Hotel and then at the Plaza.

"What I gave up for Zelda was women," he'd written Dr. Oscar Forel, the leading psychiatrist at Prangins Clinic in Switzerland, in 1930, "and it wasn't easy in the position my success gave me." Now, on his own, he felt free to pursue women.

Ledger entry for March 1934: "Parker and O'Hara." With Fitzgerald in town, Parker asked him to join her, John O'Hara, and O'Hara's former wife, Helen, for an evening out. Scott, under the influence, began making passes at Helen during the cab ride taking her home and, barely able to walk, accompanied her inside her apartment house. "He was awful," Parker told O'Hara. "Why didn't you punch him?" Well, O'Hara said, he didn't really have any rights in the matter, and Helen seemed to be enjoying the attention. It may be, too, that the aspiring Irish-American writer did not want to alienate the older and more successful Irish-American one. When Fitzgerald sent him an advance copy of *Tender Is the Night*, O'Hara told him that "the little [they had] talked in New York" had enabled O'Hara to finish his own *Appointment in Samarra*, his first and best novel. At the time, O'Hara wrote, he'd felt "bushed, as Dottie says," was nearly broke, and about ready to say the hell with his book until Fitzgerald "talked to [him] and seemed to accept [him]."

During his time in New York, Fitzgerald arranged for an exhibition of Zelda's paintings by the art dealer Cary Ross. Thirteen paintings and fifteen drawings were shown at his studio from 29 March through 30 April, with a small supplementary display in the lobby of the Algonquin. Accompanied by a nurse, Zelda came down for the opening, saw an exhibition of Georgia O'Keeffe's work, attended a luncheon Scribner put on to celebrate her exhibition and the publication of *Tender Is the Night*, and became hysterical on the train ride back to Craig House.

The *New Yorker* and *Time* both ran articles on the exhibition. "Last week, Zelda Fitzgerald showed her pictures, made her latest bid for fame. . . . [She] was hoping her pictures would gratify her great ambition—to earn her own living," the *Time* article concluded. On a financial basis, however, the show was not a success. Eight watercolor drawings were sold, and one oil painting. All of them were purchased by friends of the Fitzgeralds. The Murphys bought the oil, *Chinese Theater*, for two hundred dollars. An accomplished painter himself, Gerald described the acrobats it depicted as "hideous men, all red with swollen, intertwining legs . . . figures out of a nightmare, monstrous and morbid." The watercolors brought in about fifteen dollars apiece. They were "pitifully inexpensive," said Dorothy Parker, who bought two of them: a portrait of Scott called *The Cornet Player*, and one of a dancer who looks like Zelda working out at the barre. Parker knew she would never hang them: "There was that blood red color she used and the painful, miserable quality of emotion behind the paintings." But she was deeply sympathetic with Zelda's misfortune and gave her a book that she thought might comfort her. It did not. In a letter to Scott from Craig House, Zelda complains that she couldn't stand "the pseudo-noble-simplicity of that book Dorothy P. gave me."

One of the most interesting of her paintings depicts Scott wearing a crown of thorns. James Thurber, who went to see her show, characterized it as "a sharp, warm, ironic study of her husband's handsome and sensitive profile." A few nights later he met Fitzgerald himself, for the first time, at Tony's, a speakeasy on 52nd Street. The two writers drank and talked for hours. Fitzgerald struck Thurber as "witty, forlorn, pathetic, romantic, worried, hopeful and despondent"—fearful that his talent might "be lost like his watch, or mislaid like his hat, or slowly depleted like his bank account."

He was also, it turned out, badly in need of women, even just to talk to. Around three a.m. he asked Thurber if he knew of "a good girl" they could call on. Thurber telephoned an actress he knew, she agreed to the visit, and the two men stayed at her apartment until dawn, with Fitzgerald talking on and on and passing her catalogues of his wife's exhibit. For his article about that night, Thurber borrowed the title of Zelda's portrait—"Scott in Thorns."

Fitzgerald stayed in New York until mid-May. Unhappy with the reviews of *Tender Is the Night*, he was drinking hard and looking for sexual satisfaction. Staying at the Plaza Hotel, he became involved in a "crazy" week with a touring group of female acrobats. And if there was indeed "a one or two night" affair with Parker, Fitzgerald's *Ledger* entry for May, "Dotty Parker in hotel," strongly suggests that it happened at that time.

Fitzgerald biographer André LeVot described the affair as "a fleeting encounter between two troubled souls" and proposed that Fitzgerald went into it more out of despair and Parker more out of compassion than either of them out of love or desire. As a fellow alcoholic, Parker could feel sorry for what Fitzgerald was going through, but, according to Marion Meade, she also "despised in him" the same self-pity, lack of discipline, and waste of talent she hated in herself. Besides, Parker was living with Alan Campbell at the time. If indeed they slept together, Meade believed, both of them must have been drunk.

Back in Baltimore, Scott apparently tried at least once more to arrange a rendezvous with Parker. Early in July 1934, he sent a telegram to her New York address, not knowing that she and Campbell had left for Denver, where he was to play in summer stock. The couple's arrival caused a considerable stir in that western city. In New York they could live together without outraging the citizenry. In Denver they were castigated for "living in sin." Campbell compounded the problem by telling reporters they were married. The wire services established that they were not, and, on the evening of 18 June, the couple drove across the state line to New Mexico, where a local justice of the peace made an "honest" woman out of Parker. So when Fitzgerald tried to get in touch with Parker—his telegram has not been located—she wired him back on 6 July.

DEAR SCOTT THEY JUST FORWARDED YOUR WIRE BUT LOOK WHERE I
AM ALL MARRIED TO ALAN CAMPBELL AND EVERYTHING. ALAN PLAY-
ING STOCK HERE FOR SUMMER. DEEPEST LOVE AND ALL THOUGHTS
ALWAYS FROM BOTH OF US.

They would not meet again until three years later, in Hollywood.

1937–1940: HOLLYWOOD

Fitzgerald's life and career bottomed out during 1935 and 1936. With his drinking out of control, he was several times hospitalized or placed in the care of a
registered nurse. He could no longer produce the stories of young love that the
Saturday Evening Post paid premium prices for. The three "Crack-Up" articles
for *Esquire* in the spring of 1936, detailing his personal downfall, represented
his major achievement during that period but sent the wrong message to the
literary marketplace.

His agent, Harold Ober, came to the rescue, negotiating a contract with
Metro-Goldwyn-Mayer that would pay Fitzgerald one thousand dollars a
week as a screenwriter. He arrived in Hollywood early in July 1937, seeking a
fresh start and struggling to maintain his sobriety. The man who got off the
train, pale and haggard, looked like a shadow of his former self. Ring Lardner
Jr. could hardly believe the change in personality from the "brash, cheerful,
optimistic, ambitious, driving young man" he'd known in Great Neck to the
"withdrawn, very quiet, shy man that he had become."

Ober steered Fitzgerald to the Garden of Allah, a hotel–apartment complex
in West Hollywood where many movie people occupied rooms or bunga-
lows. Several were writer friends of Fitzgerald's, including Marc Connelly,
John O'Hara, Robert Benchley, and Parker and Campbell, who had come to
Hollywood late in 1934 and by 1937 were established as a crack screenwriting
team commanding twenty-five hundred dollars a week.

"The precious lazybones," Fitzgerald called Parker, but if that was true of
her as a writer, she was anything but lazy in her devotion to left-wing causes.
Her political awakening had started a decade earlier, when she went to Boston
to march in protest against the 1927 execution of the anarchists Nicola Sacco
and Bartolomeo Vanzetti and managed to get herself arrested and fined five
dollars for "loitering and sauntering." After that, she declared that her "heart
and soul" were with the cause of socialism.

In Hollywood she played a leading role in the Screen Writers Guild, opposing the exploitation of most writers by producers—never mind the rare ones who were earning princely salaries. Union, she proudly observed, was not a four-letter word. She was also a founder of Hollywood's Anti-Nazi League, routinely signed appeals for Communist or Communist-front organizations, and in some cases helped to raise funds for them. These activities led to an investigation by the FBI—her file ran to nine hundred pages—but only one public interrogation. Asked if she had ever been a member of the Communist Party of the United States, Parker evoked her Fifth Amendment right and declined to answer.

Fitzgerald, too, shifted to the left during the 1930s, when in the trough of the Depression it seemed that capitalism was doomed and Communism destined to replace it. He read and recommended to Zelda a primer on the Soviet five-year plan early in the decade. Later, living in Baltimore, he took political lessons from the charismatic Communist V. F. Calverton, editor of the *Modern Quarterly*. In meetings with another Communist, union leader Jay Lovestone, Fitzgerald briefly considered founding a radical magazine of his own.

In June 1937, the month before he left for Hollywood, Fitzgerald went to New York to attend the second American Writers Congress, a Popular Front organization. Donald Ogden Stewart presided over the meeting. Featured speaker Ernest Hemingway challenged the writers in the audience to stop sitting around debating abstruse points of political doctrine, get off their duffs, and go to Spain to aid the anti-Fascist Republicans in the Spanish Civil War.

Fitzgerald, as well as Parker and Campbell, were among the left-wingers invited to the home of actors Fredric March and Florence Eldridge on 12 July 1937, when Hemingway and the Dutch Communist filmmaker Joris Ivens screened the final cut of *The Spanish Earth*, the propaganda film directed by Ivens and shot in Spain on behalf of the Republican cause, with much of it written and narrated by Hemingway. In the film's most frightening scene, terrified children are depicted looking at the sky and shouting "Aviacion," as German planes above them unload their bombs. In response to an appeal from Hemingway, several Hollywood luminaries, Parker among them, contributed one thousand dollars each, a sum that he guaranteed would put an ambulance on the ground within a month to care for soldiers and civilians wounded by the Fascists.

Parker and Campbell invited a number of the attendees to repair to their place for a nightcap, an occasion inventively recalled in Hellman's best-selling *An Unfinished Woman*. Fitzgerald gave her a ride to the party, Hellman wrote, crouched over the wheel with trembling hands and driving so slowly down Sunset Boulevard that passing cars honked and drivers leaned out to shout at them. When they arrived, Fitzgerald told her he was reluctant to confront Hemingway, now that he was sober and shaky and Hemingway a famous and dominant presence. "It's a long story, Ernest and me," he said, and indeed it was. Hellman told Fitzgerald he mustn't be afraid, took his arm, and ushered him inside. Just as they entered the living room, Hemingway threw his high-ball glass against the stone fireplace.

Parker, in the kitchen, missed this display. "Hemingway smashed his glass in the fireplace," Hellman told her. "Of course," Parker answered, and went on unloading ice cubes. The incident increased Fitzgerald's anxiety, and Hellman tried unsuccessfully to enlist Dashiell Hammett—who was to be her long-time lover—to reassure him. Presumably Scott went home alone, still in awe or terror of Hemingway, a man he had once thought of as his best friend. It was later that night, according to Hellman's memoir, that in a confidential woman-to-woman conversation Parker told her about her brief affair with Fitzgerald "some years before."

So there it is—the one source behind the widespread assumption that Fitz-gerald and Parker, at least fleetingly, were lovers. Perhaps it hardly mattered as compared with what happened a few nights later, when Parker introduced Fitzgerald to Sheilah Graham, the English-born columnist who became his lover and companion for the rest of his life.

Still, a biographer wants to come as close as possible to the truth, and that depends in good part on whether one can trust Hellman as a source. The quick and easy answer to that question is no. Much of what she wrote about the night of 12 July 1937 is demonstrably untrue. She herself wrote that she met Hemingway for the first time a few months later. Nor was Fitzgerald so apprehensive about seeing Hemingway as she maintained. He and Hem-ingway had had a pleasant lunch earlier that day with Benchley, and the next morning Scott sent Ernest a congratulatory telegram reading:

THE PICTURE WAS BEYOND PRAISE AND SO WAS YOUR ATTITUDE.

Like many creative writers, when writing about herself, Hellman shaped the narrative as she went along. Norman Mailer maintained that Hellman "didn't know the boundary between fact and fiction," or, if she did know, decided to ignore it. Martha Gellhorn, incensed by Hellman's portrayal of herself as an intrepid war correspondent greatly admired by Hemingway, accused her of being an "apocryphiar" in a *Paris Review* article. On television's *Dick Cavett Show*, Mary McCarthy famously declared that every word Hellman uttered was a lie, including "and" and "the," eliciting a lawsuit that remained unsettled when McCarthy died. Hellman saw to it that she emerged as an admirable figure in *An Unfinished Woman*—hadn't she been kind and understanding in helping Fitzgerald fight off his demons?—and also in two succeeding book/memoirs she wrote, *Pentimento* and *Scoundrel Time*. But there was little self-aggrandizement to be gained from repeating (or inventing) a confession by Parker about an affair with Fitzgerald.

In Hollywood the strong political sympathies she and Parker shared enabled them to become long-lasting friends, despite Hellman's domineering nature and spells of outright nastiness. Both of them followed Hemingway's example by traveling to Spain in late 1937. Parker and Campbell were in Valencia one Sunday morning when that city, the capital of Republican Spain, suffered its worst bombing attack of the war. Dorothy ventured out afterward to see the damage—piles of rubble supporting a broken doll and a dead kitten, two small girls pushing past guards to the bombed-out house where their mother may have died.

That night she and Alan went to a café where the waiter proudly presented them with a few pieces of grayish ice for their vermouth. They got to talking with six Loyalist soldiers on a few hours' pass from their unit. Tired and dusty, the soldiers told them about not being able to write home for fear that their letters would be intercepted by the Fascists and their families ostracized or worse. When the men had to return to duty, she and Alan gave them all the cigarettes they had, fourteen cigarettes for six men. Then everyone stood up, said "Salud" back and forth, and the men filed out of the café. When Campbell summoned the waiter for the bill a little later, he shook his head and moved away. "The soldiers had paid for [their] drinks." Or so Parker wrote as the final one-sentence paragraph of "Soldiers of the Republic," her story that appeared in the 8 February 1938 issue of the *New Yorker*.

In Hollywood during 1938, Hellman and Parker worked together to fight off a challenge to the Screen Writers Guild from a competing union created by producers in an attempt to undermine the hard-lining Guild. They remained active in the Hollywood Anti-Nazi League, and both of them became members of the Communist Party.

Fitzgerald, not much of a joiner, did not go nearly as far in his political activities. He was having trouble enough of his own during 1937-40, occasionally falling off the wagon with disastrous consequences (as at the Dartmouth winter carnival with Budd Schulberg), failing to get his contract renewed with MGM, and, though he worked hard at the craft, earning but a single screen credit (for *Three Comrades*) over the three-year period.

Fitzgerald continued to admire Parker as a short-story writer, recommending her work to daughter Scottie when she was still in prep school. "I am glad you have gotten around to liking Dorothy Parker and that you had the good taste to pick out her 'Diary of a New York Lady,'" he wrote Scottie early in 1938. He thought that story, a clever monologue uncovering the shallowness and self-absorption of a New York society woman, was one of Parker's best.

He knew, also, from a 1935 fan letter from English novelist G. B. (Gladys Bronwyn) Stern, that Parker was an enthusiastic advocate for *Tender Is the Night*. She and Parker were talking about the novel, Stern writes, "and what a magnificent piece of work it was . . . and how it turned us inside out when we read and didn't put us back again and what lovely sensitive writing was in it."

Nonetheless he was to some degree envious of the Parker-Campbell team's success. In a 14 September 1940 letter to Gerald Murphy, he categorized everyone in Hollywood as either corrupt or "supremely indifferent." He listed Parker, one of the movie capital's "spoiled writers," among the indifferent and had his doubts about her conversion to Communism: "That Dotty has embraced [that] church and reads her office faithfully every day does not affect her indifference." In that same week, though, he sounded a different note in a letter to Scottie, about to begin her freshman year at Vassar: "You will notice that there is a strongly organized left-wing movement there. I do not particularly want you to think about politics, but I do not want you to set yourself against this movement. I am known as a left-wing sympathizer and would be proud if you were. In any case, I should feel outraged if you identified yourself with Nazism or Red-baiting in any form. Some of those radical girls may not look like much now but in your lifetime they are liable to be high in the councils of the nation."

The Last Tycoon revealed some of Fitzgerald's political ambivalence. Monroe Stahr, the protagonist/hero of that unfinished novel, seeks to produce artistically good, even great films. In excellent "process" scenes, Fitzgerald displays Stahr's genius in action, as he guides writers and directors and actors toward that goal. But Stahr also regards these men and women as expendable, pawns for him to use or discard as necessary. This leads to a confrontation with the union leader Brimmer, a dedicated young Communist who debates Stahr and then knocks him down. The producer's worst enemy, though, is the company executive Earl Brady, a representative of the money men interested only in the bottom line who owned the Hollywood studios. They want Stahr to make popular movies, never mind how trashy and sentimental, and are ready to fire him if he does not. Fitzgerald's novel-in-progress placed his protagonist in the middle between opposing forces of communism and capitalism. Fitzgerald had not yet figured out how to resolve that dilemma for himself when he died of a heart attack in Sheilah Graham's ground-floor apartment on 21 December 1940.

During his last year, he and Sheilah had been leading a quiet life as he worked steadily on *The Last Tycoon*. He "was going into society for the first time in some months," he wrote Zelda on 28 September, to attend a tea "at Dottie Parker's (Mrs. Alan Campbell) for Don Stewart's ex-wife [Beatrice], the Countess Tolstoy."

Fitzgerald and Parker met for the last time at a dinner party on Friday, the thirteenth of December 1940, at the home of Nathanael and Eileen West. Elliot Paul was there, along with screenwriters Frances Goodrich and Albert Hackett. At the end of the evening the mood grew nostalgic, and they sang "The Last Time I Saw Paris." Eight days later Fitzgerald died. Nine days later West died in an automobile accident. The superstitious Campbell, mindful of the Friday-the-thirteenth pattern of bad luck in threes, was terrified that he would be next.

In her 1956 "Writers at Work" interview for the *Paris Review*, Parker bitterly reflected on her years in Hollywood. "It was a horror to me when I was there and it's a horror to look back on," she said. It wasn't that the work destroyed the artist's talent. "Garbage though they turn[ed] out, Hollywood writers [weren't] writing down": they were doing their best. And the problem wasn't the money, even if she thought Hollywood money was really "congealed snow" that melted in your hands. No, it was the people who made the place so awful. The worst she could think of was "the director who put his finger in Scott Fitzgerald's face and complained, 'Pay you. Why, you ought to pay us.' And it wasn't only the people, but the indignity to which your ability was put. It was terrible about Scott; if you'd seen him you'd have been sick. When he died no one came to the funeral, not a single soul came, or even sent a flower. I said, 'Poor son of a bitch,' a quote right out of *The Great*

Gatsby, and everyone thought it was another wisecrack. But it was said in dead seriousness."

Parker's memory of Fitzgerald's death was not quite accurate. There was no memorial service in California. Instead, his remains were laid out for viewing at the mortuary. The corpse had been doctored to look like a Hollywood B production. There wasn't a line on the face, a gray hair on the head, but the hands were "horribly wrinkled and thin": testimony that "despite all the props of youth," Fitzgerald had died, at forty-four, "an old man." Very few came to see the corpse. Parker looked at it a long time—and then made her valedictory remark.

The body was shipped to Baltimore for funeral and burial. Zelda attended, and therefore Sheilah Graham could not. At a party she and Campbell gave on Christmas day, Dorothy could see how upset Sheilah was. So she left her other guests, guided her to the bedroom, made her lie down, stayed with her, and cried with her. The two women said their farewells together.

To answer Bryer's query, then: I think Fitzgerald and Parker were briefly lovers in May 1934, but no, there is no "firm evidence" about that. (Corrigan omitted the claim from her book on *Gatsby*.) But they definitely were friends who cared about each other and colleagues who valued each other's work. In 1945 Parker played a role in the revival of Fitzgerald's reputation. She edited *The Portable F. Scott Fitzgerald* for Viking, assembling *Gatsby*, *Tender*, and some stories in one convenient volume. That book acquainted many readers with his fiction for the first time, myself among them. "All Fitzgerald was," John O'Hara wrote in the introduction, "was our best novelist, one of our best novellaists, and one of our finest writers of short stories." That sounded like an extravagant exaggeration in 1945. It doesn't sound that way seventy years later.

FIVE

A Fitzgerald Autobiography

The promotional copy on the back cover of *The Crack-Up*, which Edmund Wilson brought out in 1945, hailed the book as a virtual Fitzgerald autobiography. This claim (which is no longer made in current printings) launched the book under false colors, for in it Wilson collected a number of items that were written not by F. Scott Fitzgerald but to him or about him by Gertrude Stein, Edith Wharton, T. S. Eliot, Thomas Wolfe, John Dos Passos, Paul Rosenfeld, Glenway Wescott, John Peale Bishop, and Wilson himself. The names of these illustrious literary figures on the title page served to testify to the distinction of a writer whose reputation at that time was by no means secure. Presumably Wilson included a sizable sampling from Fitzgerald's notebooks for a similar reason: as evidence that his former Princeton friend was a serious craftsman and not merely, to quote the jacket puffery of the most recent printing, "a man whose personality still charms us all and whose reckless gaiety and genius made him a living symbol of the Jazz Age." The notebook entries—more than 150 pages worth—provide interesting clues to Fitzgerald's working habits. They rarely tell us much about the rest of his life.

The more modest claim (from the latest printing) that *The Crack-Up* represents an "extraordinary autobiographical collection" rests on the inclusion of the three "Crack-Up" articles together with several other essays he wrote between 1931 and 1937. These take up about 75 pages, less than one-fourth of what is otherwise a mishmash of laudatory letters, patronizing criticism, and writerly notes, the whole sandwiched between a poem from Wilson that damns Fitzgerald as a barely competent drunk and one by Bishop that pictures him in the lower depths. Not included among the autobiographical essays, moreover, are any of those that Fitzgerald wrote in the 1920s; several extremely significant pieces from the 1930s—some presented in the guise of fiction—are also left out.

Despite the considerable volume of posthumously published Fitzgerald material, there exists no single book that begins to approach an autobiography. To put such a book together would involve picking up the essays in *The Crack-Up*, adding a number of items from Arthur Mizener's selections in *Afternoon of an Author* (1957), adding contributions from *F. Scott Fitzgerald in His Own Time*, edited by Matthew J. Bruccoli and Jackson R. Bryer (1971) and from *The Stories of F. Scott Fitzgerald* (1951), and rescuing into book form a few pieces that are so far available only in old magazines. Such a collection would do justice to Fitzgerald and make a contribution to our understanding of him, his writing, and his time.

Fitzgerald himself twice suggested to Maxwell Perkins at Scribner that a collection of his nonfiction be published, first in 1934 and again two years later. The two proposals were substantially different. It was Scribner's practice to bring out a second book by its authors in the wake of a novel—story collections had succeeded each of Fitzgerald's first three novels—so the subject on the table when Fitzgerald wrote Perkins on 15 May 1934, a month after the publication of *Tender Is the Night*, was "what next?" Fitzgerald advanced four plans for a follow-up book: (1) an omnibus including new stories and the pick of earlier story collections; (2) a gathering of his nine Basil and five Josephine stories, all written between 1928 and 1931; (3) a selection of new short stories drawn from the forty or so he had written between 1926 and 1934; and (4) a collection of autobiographical nonfiction somewhat along the lines of Alexander Woollcott's chatty and engaging *While Rome Burns*, then making a success in the marketplace (Kuehl and Bryer 195-98).

"We are strongly in favor of Plan #2, Basil and Josephine" and "[a]fter Plan #2, we favor Plan #3," Perkins wrote back (198-99). After some delay, plan 3 prevailed, and the story collection *Taps at Reveille* was published in March 1935. As for plan 4, Fitzgerald's proposal for a book of personal essays, Perkins dismissed it out of hand, without so much as a word of comment or explanation. Considering the matter retrospectively, it is easy to see why.

In presenting the idea for such a collection, Fitzgerald more or less undermined his own proposal. He began by acknowledging that he had reserved most of his "personal stuff" for his fiction, but then went on to insist—three times in two paragraphs, clearly protesting too much—that "a good many of my articles and random pieces have *attracted a really quite wide attention*," that two 1924 contributions to the *Saturday Evening Post* ("How to Live on $36,000 a Year" and "How to Live on Practically Nothing a Year") "*attracted such wide attention* in their day that I have yet to hear the last of them," and that a number of other articles had also "*attracted attention*." In the first paragraph, he also raised the basic problems of unity and timeliness: without "a tie-up of title and matter" the volume might "look like a collection of what the cat brought in," and "in a changing world" it might seem "hilariously dated" (Kuehl and Bryer 197; emphasis added).

Neither of these problems disappeared as Fitzgerald summoned from memory the probable contents of his nonfiction book. Most of them harked back to the boom years of the 1920s, when he alternately presented himself in popular magazines as a romantic genius who could casually toss off stories and novels and as an authority on flappers and sheiks, modern marriage and child-rearing. But there were also a few more recent, serious essays— in particular "Echoes of the Jazz Age" (1931), "One Hundred False Starts" (1933), "Ring" (1934), and "My Lost City" (sold to *Cosmopolitan* in 1933 but not published until 1945, in *The Crack-Up*). The volume could be padded out, Fitzgerald suggested, with what he called "hors d'oeuvres," "short sketches," "some light verse," a couple of articles he and Zelda had collaborated on, and a few stories he'd written at twelve and thirteen years of age. The result might indeed resemble something the cat dragged in, and even with ephemera added to the mix, Fitzgerald feared his collection might run too short to sell. He had not actually seen Woollcott's book, he wrote Perkins, and did not know how thick it was. The one he was proposing did not seem "very voluminous" (Kuehl and Bryer 198).

Probably Fitzgerald would not have made this halfhearted proposal had he not been eager to convert anything and everything he'd written into cash. As was often the case during his career, he was relying on loans from those who believed in him—editor Perkins and agent Harold Ober—to stay financially afloat. At the end of the 15 May letter, for example, Fitzgerald thanked Perkins for depositing $600 in his bank account, and little over a month later he sent his editor "a begging telegram" for a thousand dollars. He could not understand how he had gotten so deeply in debt, he maintained (Kuehl and Bryer 202). He had been writing and selling stories since the publication of

Tender, after all, and had even sold "some of Zelda's little articles"—"Show Mr. and Mrs. F. to Number—" and "Auction—Model 1934"—to *Esquire* for $200 apiece, no more than a pittance compared with the $3,000 that mass-circulation magazines like the *Post* and *McCall's* were paying for his stories. "I have got to get myself out of this morass of debt," he wrote Perkins in August (Kuehl and Bryer 206), but the money situation actually worsened in the two years ahead. His income dropped from about $20,000 in 1934 to less than $17,000 the following year and barely $10,000 in 1936, his lowest income since he had cast his lot as a professional writer (FSF, *Ledger* 74-76). He did not reduce his expenses accordingly. During much of 1935 and 1936, Fitzgerald stayed at the elegant and not inexpensive Grove Park Inn in Asheville while paying Zelda's medical expenses and Scottie's school bills. At the same time, his health was deteriorating, his drinking drifting out of control, and his ability to churn out high-paying fiction dwindling away.

Fitzgerald first came to western North Carolina in February 1935, when he spent a month at the Oak Hall Hotel in Tryon, a Blue Ridge Mountains resort community south of Asheville where Lefty and Nora Flynn lived. Fitzgerald may or may not have had an affair with Nora—Edmund Wilson thought he had (Meyers 252)—but certainly he admired her exuberance and style. Nora was the youngest of the five prominent Langhorne sisters of Virginia. Among her older sisters was Nancy, Lady Astor, who became the first woman in Parliament. The Langhorne women were blessed with beauty, vitality, and charm, but Nora was the rebel of the group (Meyers 251-52). In particular, she shocked the family by leaving the husband and children of her first marriage to run away with Flynn, a former Yale football star and cowboy actor. As Fitzgerald depicted her in "The Intimate Strangers," a story he concocted from the Flynns' experience for the June 1935 *McCall's,* "life crowded into her voice, a spiced voice with a lot of laughter, a little love, much quiet joy and an awful sympathy for people in it" (FSF, *Price* 609). Undoubtedly Nora was a good influence on Fitzgerald. A Christian Scientist, she did not herself drink and had rescued her husband from alcoholism. But she could not cure Fitzgerald or protect him from the troubles that lay ahead.

When *Taps at Reveille* came out in late March, reviews quite sensibly noted the uneven quality of the contents. The book did not sell well. On a return visit to Baltimore, an X-ray exam revealed a tubercular cavity in Fitzgerald's left lung. What he needed was mountain air, his doctor advised. So Fitzgerald returned to Asheville for the summer, leaving Zelda at Sheppard-Pratt

Hospital and Scottie in the care of Isabelle Owens. The climate in North Carolina may have been salubrious. Fitzgerald's behavior was not.

The events of that summer were recorded by two acquaintances Fitzgerald made during his stay. According to Tony Buttitta, who was running a bookstore in downtown Asheville, Fitzgerald smoked continually, drank to excess, ate almost nothing, took Luminal in order to sleep, and sometimes broke into tears like "an overwrought, indulged child" (qtd. in Meyers 254). Broken down though he may have been, Fitzgerald managed to carry on a reckless affair with Beatrice Dance, a wealthy young married woman who was also staying at the Grove Park Inn. Buttitta's memoir presents many of the details of this affair. An even fuller account appears in the journal of Laura Guthrie, who met Fitzgerald when she was reading palms for guests at the inn. Fitzgerald had his palm read and subsequently attempted to seduce her. Although initially smitten and driven "nearly crazy" (qtd. in SD 131) by her yearning, Guthrie refused to succumb. Instead she became his secretary and confidante for the rest of the summer. She also served as a go-between in the affair with Beatrice Dance, which began in mid-June and lasted until Dance's husband and family doctor stopped it in early August.

The aftershock was drastic for Dance, who suffered a nervous breakdown. Fitzgerald, less troubled, was nonetheless saddened by the end of the affair. Dance had proposed that they run away together. She had plenty of money to pay off his debts and support them both, she said. For a time, she restored a trace of his youthful vitality and made him feel that a viable future lay ahead (Buttitta 80).

Vitality was precisely what Fitzgerald lacked. He simply did not have the energy—the mental speed and drive—to write successful fiction, an unfortunate condition that was exacerbated by his drinking. He began the summer on a "no hard liquor" regimen, consuming vast quantities of beer instead. It ran down his throat like a waterfall down a rock, Guthrie observed. He switched back to gin in September, leading her to conclude that "being tied to an alcoholic whether as secretary, nurse, or wife" constituted the hardest work in the world. "I never felt less in love with a man in my life," she confided to her diary when she put him in the hospital on Friday the 13th (qtd. in SD 132).

But it was not liquor alone that kept him from writing. In "One Hundred False Starts," a March 1933 essay for the *Post*, Fitzgerald sketched out some of the difficulties. The piece begins with references to humorous entries in the "leather-bound wastebasket" he fatuously calls his "notebook" (FSF, *After-noon* 127). There he supposedly finds a note that reads, in its entirety, "Boopsie Dee was cute," and can summon up no recollection of where that "preposter-ous statement" was supposed to lead. As the essay proceeds, Fitzgerald's tone becomes less facetious. He has trouble conceiving plots, he confesses, and the basic problem is that he cannot convert what happens to other people into story form: "Mostly, we authors must repeat ourselves. . . . We have two or three great and moving experiences in our lives—experiences so great and moving that it doesn't seem at the time that anyone else has been so caught up and pounded and dazzled and astonished and beaten and broken and rescued and illumi-nated and rewarded and humbled in just that way ever before" (132).

So authors tell those two or three stories over and over again, "each time in a new disguise." Fitzgerald could find a thousand plots in any criminal law library, but they would not work for him. "Whether it's something that hap-pened twenty years ago or only yesterday," he writes, "I must start out with an emotion—one that's close to me and that I can understand" (132).

In order to succeed, then, fiction had to be grounded in a writer's own experience and deepest feelings, a point he underlined in his October 1933 memorial essay on Ring Lardner (Wilson 34-40). The two writers had become friends and drinking companions in 1921, at a time when Lardner seemed pos-sessed of "an abundance of quiet vitality" (34). But he was dogged even then by "the impenetrable despair" that pursued him to his death. In effect—and Fitzgerald must have sensed this—in chronicling Lardner's descent into sleep-lessness and depression and despair, he was writing about what threatened to become of himself and foreshadowing the confessional essays ahead, par-ticularly "Sleeping and Waking" (December 1934) and the three "Crack-Up" articles of early 1936. In his reminiscence, he reprimands Lardner for with-holding too much of himself from his work. Once he had suggested to Lardner that he should take the time to write "something deeply personal," but Lard-ner would not do that. At a crucial period in his life, Fitzgerald wrote, Lardner had formed the habit of not revealing himself. According to his lights, it simply was not done. But as a consequence, Fitzgerald points out, Lardner got less of what was in his mind and heart down on paper "than any other American of the first flight" (Wilson 38). It was a shame, and a mistake that Fitzgerald did not intend to make.

The trouble was that by 1935 he was no longer able to infuse his fiction with the emotional power he had once commanded. Desperately searching for material, he tried a series about a father and daughter—the Gwen stories—and launched his medieval Count of Darkness yarns, but these did not measure up to his usual standard. In his 1951 collection of Fitzgerald's best stories, Cowley included nothing written between 1933 and 1937. Fitzgerald's well was running dry. As he observed in his notebooks, there seemed less weather than in his youth, and hardly any "men and women at all" (Wilson 128).

So in November 1935 he tried something different. He came back to the mountains, holing up this time in the Skylands Hotel in Hendersonville, Tennessee. Arnold Gingrich at *Esquire* had provided him with a mantra to break his writer's block. He was to repeat over and over, "I can't write stories of young love for *The Saturday Evening Post* because I can't write stories of young love for *The Saturday Evening Post* because . . . " and so on (qtd. in Potts 88). In Hendersonville, Fitzgerald wrote his "Crack-Up" articles instead, articles that amply demonstrated *why* he could not go on writing stories of young love for the *Saturday Evening Post*.

In a notebook entry, he emphasized how cheaply he was living and how strapped he was for funds: "Monday and Tuesday I had two tins of potted meat, three oranges and a box of Uneedas [biscuits] and two cans of beer. For the food, that totalled eighteen cents a day" (Wilson 232). It amused him that the deferential clerk downstairs did not know he was "tens of thousands of dollars in debt" and had less than forty cents cash in his pocket. The Flynns wondered why he did not just "jump into a taxi" and run over to Tryon for dinner, but that would have cost four dollars he didn't have (Wilson 252-53). Nora came to see him instead at his "frightful hotel," where she found him drunk and ill and "thinking about himself, as usual" (qtd. in Meyers 260). But at least he was turning that self-consciousness to account.

Fitzgerald earned $250 apiece for the three "Crack-Up" pieces that ran in the February, March, and April numbers of *Esquire*. As confessional essays, they seem tame indeed when compared to the jarringly candid memoirs of the 1990s and 2000s. In writing of his personal breakdown Fitzgerald held a good deal back, particularly where liquor and sex were concerned. Yet at the time, his articles were regarded as startlingly forthright. Too much so, most of his literary connections felt. "I think those confounded *Esquire* articles have done you a great deal of harm and I hope you won't do any more," advised Ober (qtd. in Mellow 453), who was trying to sell his client's services to Hollywood. Perkins also disapproved of the essays—gentlemen did not talk about themselves in public—yet found a ray of hopefulness in the darkness, for, as he saw it, "a hopeless man" would not have bothered to write them (qtd. in Mellow 445).

John Dos Passos and Ernest Hemingway took stronger adversarial positions. "Christ, man," Dos Passos scolded Fitzgerald, "how do you find time in the middle of the general conflagration to worry about all that stuff?" They were living through one of history's most tragic moments, he asserted, and Fitzgerald's private collapse looked mighty insignificant. If he wanted to write about cracking up, why did he not do it in a novel (as, of course, he had done in *Tender Is the Night*) instead of "spilling it in little pieces for Arnold Gingrich" (qtd. in Mellow 445-46)? Hemingway's criticism was more indirect but at least as hurtful. Fitzgerald was wallowing in "the shamelessness of defeat" (qtd. in Mellow 446), he wrote Perkins. He had always known that Fitzgerald could not think, Hemingway added, but he did have a marvelous talent and should use it instead of whining in public. Then Hemingway himself sat down to write "The Snows of Kilimanjaro," a masterly story about a failed writer for the August 1936 *Esquire* that pointedly referred to "poor Scott Fitzgerald" and how he had been "wrecked" by his obsession with the rich. He figured it was "open season" on his old friend once he had spilled his guts in *Esquire*, Hemingway explained to Perkins. There was also a backdoor attack in a letter from Hemingway to Dos Passos, in which he passed on word from Perkins that Fitzgerald seemed to have "many imaginary diseases along with, I imagine, some very real liver trouble" (qtd. in Reynolds 227).

Gingrich did not share the prevailing view that the essays hurt Fitzgerald's career. The "Crack-Up" pieces produced nasty letters from Dos and Hem, he acknowledged, and, even worse, stimulated Michel Mok, a reporter from the *New York Post*, to track Fitzgerald to the Grove Park Inn on his fortieth birthday (24 September 1936) and write a devastating account of a drunken and self-pitying author "engulfed in despair" (Bruccoli and Bryer 299). Still, Gingrich argued, bad publicity was better than no publicity at all. Having hit bottom, Fitzgerald's stock could only go up. The brouhaha caused by the *Esquire* articles "undoubtedly reminded Hollywood that he was still around," Gingrich felt (qtd. in Meyers 264), and led directly or indirectly to his lucrative contract with MGM in July 1937.

Ober would certainly have disagreed with that conclusion. But in fact the first two "Crack-Up" essays—"The Crack-Up" and "Pasting It Together"— did elicit a letter from Simon and Schuster proposing that Fitzgerald publish a volume of autobiographical sketches. Armed with this leverage, Fitzgerald wrote Perkins on 25 March 1936 with a reminder that two years earlier he had proposed gathering up his "definitely autobiographical" nonfiction and had been turned down. He was aware that unity posed a problem and that some of his pieces might seem dated: the book would have to be "somehow joined together." His new model was no longer Woollcott's rather insubstantial *While Rome Burns*. Now he cited Gertrude Stein's *The Autobiography of Alice B. Toklas*, a work of undoubted literary importance, as the sort of thing he had in mind. There was really a lot of material he could include, Fitzgerald pointed out. Besides, the *Esquire* articles had stirred up considerable interest. Of course he *wanted* to remain identified with Scribner, but if Perkins didn't like the idea, what would he "think of letting Simon and Schuster try it" (Kuehl and Bryer 227)?

Perkins replied the very next day with a significantly different idea. Did Fitzgerald recall that, when he was stalled on *Tender*, Perkins had suggested "a reminiscent book—not autobiographical, but reminiscent." Couldn't he do a book along those lines, one that would comprehend what was in the *Esquire* pieces but fold them into "a really well integrated" whole? That would be so much better than "merely to take the articles and trim them, and join them up, etc." Perkins did not elaborate on the distinction between "reminiscent" and "autobiographical," but cited as an example Fitzgerald's 1931 "Echoes of the Jazz Age," "a beautiful article" with a strong historical emphasis (Kuehl and Bryer 228). What Perkins wanted from Fitzgerald was less navel gazing and more looking outward. What he did not want was a cut-and-paste job.

"It would be one thing to join those articles together and another to write a book," Fitzgerald wrote back in mild exasperation. Then he proposed a table of contents joining together sixteen items, beginning with "Who's Who and Why" (1920), an upbeat account of how he came to write *This Side of Paradise*, and ending with the three articles about cracking up. Significantly deleted from his 1934 proposal were the ephemera: the light verse and short sketches and trivial hors d'oeuvres. He "would expect to revise" as needed and to add "some sort of telegraphic flashes" between articles, Fitzgerald added. But he did not have the time to rewrite them. He simply could not afford to do so until he pulled himself out of debt. What did Perkins think (Kuehl and Bryer 229-30)?

It would be unfortunate to do the autobiographical book now, Perkins thought, since it would cut the ground from beneath the book of reminiscence Fitzgerald could and should do later (277). A discouraged but persistent

Fitzgerald reverted to his proposal in a letter of 13 June. Gingrich had just written him that "Afternoon of an Author," scheduled for the August *Esquire*, was the best thing he had published in the six-year history of the magazine. That story and two additional ones for *Esquire*—"Author's House" and "An Author's Mother"—masqueraded as fiction but were patently autobiographical and would add ballast to the volume. Given an attractive title, he still thought the book had possibilities. He reassured Perkins that he expected to "do a certain amount of work" (230) in proof and asked him to reconsider the matter. Perkins answered with an extremely reluctant yes. He continued to think that a collection of autobiographical pieces would "injure the possibilities of a reminiscent book at some later time" (277). If Fitzgerald insisted, Perkins wrote, Scribner would publish the autobiographical book. But the editor did not really surrender. Instead he enlisted Gilbert Seldes, Fitzgerald's friend and fellow writer, to argue the case once again.

Seldes, who had written a glowing review of *The Great Gatsby*, began his letter of 23 June by telling Fitzgerald that he thought of him as "an important figure in America" who sooner or later would have to have his say, "not only in fiction but in the facts about yourself and the part you played at the beginning and what you think about it now." That book would be one of supreme importance, and to publish the raw material now, "the mere fact without the thought," would take the edge off it. Seldes knew Fitzgerald had been going through a hard time, and the recent *Esquire* pieces showed that he was moving in a thoughtful direction, though Seldes was not ready to follow him "into ruin and the rest." This was precisely the time his major book of nonfiction should be gestating, Seldes thought. It was not time "for a synthetic, put-together work" (Bruccoli and Duggan 436).

Fitzgerald took the point, and in the months ahead developed his own reasons not to do *either* a book of autobiography or of reminiscence. If the summer of 1935 was disastrous, that of 1936 was still worse. In July, he broke his collarbone diving from the high board at the Grove Park Inn. Encased in a body cast with his right arm extended, he could only dictate or write on an overhead stand. His recovery was delayed after he fell—apparently when drinking—on a trip to the bathroom and while lying on the cold tiles developed arthritis in his shoulder. He had brought Zelda to Asheville in April to undergo treatment with Dr. Robert S. Carroll at Highland Hospital. Dr. Carroll imposed a regimen of controlled diet and exercise that seemed to alleviate the suicidal mania of her last months at Sheppard-Pratt. But meeting Carroll's minimum monthly fee of $240 drove Fitzgerald deeper into debt. He owed Scribner $9,000 and Ober $11,000 at midsummer, when he secured $8,000 of what he owed Ober and $1,500 of his debt to Scribner by signing over benefits from his life insurance (Bruccoli 408-10).

His mother died on 2 September. They had never been close, but Fitzgerald felt the loss. "A most surprising thing in the death of a parent is not how little it affects you, but how much," he discovered (Bruccoli and Duggan 451). It almost seemed as if she had deserted him. In fact, Mollie McQuillan Fitzgerald left about $45,000 to be shared by Scott and his younger sister Annabel. By the time the estate was settled six months later, Fitzgerald had borrowed all but $5,000 of his half (Meyers 276-77). In the interim, Fitzgerald continued to importune Perkins and Ober—and to a lesser degree Gingrich—for advances against his inheritance and future literary output.

Scribner became understandably uneasy about such requests. Perkins talked things over with Charles Scribner, he wrote Fitzgerald on 6 October 1936, and they decided that they had to have "some business justification" before sending Fitzgerald the $2,000 he had requested by telegram. They already held a note of his for $2,000 and were disinclined to send him any more unless he would secure a guarantee from the administrator of his mother's estate that both loans would be paid from Fitzgerald's inheritance. But, Perkins went on with a trace of wistfulness, wouldn't the windfall from his mother's estate provide Fitzgerald with an interval—as long as a year, perhaps—in which he could write a book? It hardly made sense for a publishing firm to advance money to a writer who was producing nothing for them to publish. "One successful book would clear the whole slate for you all round," Perkins pointed out. Perhaps "the biographical book" (the book of reminiscence, that is) they had corresponded about would do the trick. In any case, Scribner would "feel very much better" if they knew what their author was planning (Kuehl and Bryer 232-33).

Fitzgerald's reply was not encouraging. He had "conceived" a novel for Scribner to publish, he asserted, but could not see his way clear to actually writing it. Despite his inheritance, his expenses and debts were such that he would have to go on "with this endless Post writing" (actually, the *Saturday Evening Post* was to accept only one more story of his) or else go to Hollywood to make ends meet. In any event, he was now firmly "against the autobiographical book" that had seemed so promising a few months earlier. For one thing, the *Esquire* articles would certainly have to "form part of the fabric" of the book, and "certain people" felt these had done him considerable harm (233-34). Among those people, though he did not say so, must have been Fitzgerald himself, for he knew that the "Crack-Up" pieces had generated both Hemingway's vicious slur in "The Snows of Kilimanjaro" and Michel Mok's humiliating interview. In addition, he told Perkins, his confidence that he could put together a book out of his articles had "vanished" in the face of the editor's disapproval. Any such volume would have to be made up of "miscellaneous" and "exploited" material and could hardly be expected to sell. It was not as if he were an adventurer or explorer with an incredible story to relate. Nor was he willing to "tell all" in a sensational manner. A "tell all" book might be successful financially, but would seem to put a period to his whole career. He was suffering a "general eclipse of ambition and determination and fortitude," Fitzgerald admitted. He did not know what to do next (234).

It is unfortunate that Fitzgerald neither wrote the book of reminiscence Perkins wanted nor assembled the collection of autobiographical articles he twice proposed. And it is a further misfortune that these articles have been scattered among several posthumously published collections—an unhappy situation that will be remedied in the forthcoming book edited by James L. W. West III. As Arthur Mizener commented in his introduction to *Afternoon of an Author*, Fitzgerald had an uncanny gift for combining the most deeply felt personal experience with an implicit commentary on the social and cultural and moral climate surrounding him. "However much he may be talking about himself," Mizener noted, "Fitzgerald is always talking also about a 'young American couple,' about what life in Paris or on the Riviera was like that year, about the characteristic wearing away of innocence to the point where it takes several drinks to light up the face" (3). In Emerson's terms, Fitzgerald was "a representative man," one who invariably represented both himself and his time. Even the introspective "Crack-Up" essays, as Bruce L. Grenberg has demonstrated, reveal nearly as much about the declining values of American society as about Fitzgerald's own decline.

A book of his autobiographical pieces, in other words, would have the value of illuminating much more than one life. By itself, of course, that life deserves our attention, for what Seldes said by way of argumentative flattery has become true. F. Scott Fitzgerald is an important American, one of a handful of our major twentieth-century writers. Whatever we can learn about him is worth learning.

And as we learn about Fitzgerald, we also learn about the culture he inhabited. A book of his essays about himself and his times would necessarily trace the roller-coaster shape of American life in the 1920s and 1930s. "A Fitzgerald Autobiography," as it might be called, would logically divide into three parts. Part 1, the personal pieces covering the 1920s, in which Fitzgerald conducted a jaunty "autobiographical transaction" with his audience, a willing exchange of private details for public attention (Dolan 122). Part 2, the shift in the early 1930s to a more thoughtful and problematic presentation of self as the foundations began to crumble. Part 3, his work for *Esquire* from 1936 on, where in the "Crack-Up" and "Author" essays, in "Early Success" (1937) and stories like "Financing Finnegan" (1938), he confessed how far he had fallen from the carefree days of the previous decade.

His personal trajectory, as Fitzgerald was well aware, coincided with that of the world around him: the heights of the boom years followed by a period of shocks to the system and finally the plunge into full-scale depression. As the country suffered through a series of economic blows in order to right itself, so too did Fitzgerald. Even in the darkest articles for *Esquire*, he was seeking a niche for himself as a human being and a role for himself as an artist. In his youth, success had come knocking at his door. In the mid-1930s, it seemed that the fates were marshaled against him, but he would not quite admit defeat. It would not be easy, but if he stuck to his last, if he worked hard, if he became finally a writer only, he might yet fight his way clear to recovery.

WORKS CITED

Bruccoli, Matthew J. *Some Sort of Epic Grandeur: The Life of F. Scott Fitzgerald*. New York: Harcourt Brace Jovanovich, 1981.

Bruccoli, Matthew J., and Jackson R. Bryer, eds. *F. Scott Fitzgerald in His Own Time: A Miscellany*. Kent, OH: Kent State UP, 1971.

Bruccoli, Matthew J., and Margaret M. Duggan, eds. *Correspondence of F. Scott Fitzgerald*. New York: Random House, 1980.

Buttitta, Tony. *After the Good Gay Times: Asheville Summer of '35*. New York: Viking, 1974.

Dolan, Marc. *Modern Lives: A Cultural Re-Reading of "The Lost Generation."* West Lafayette: Purdue UP, 1996.

Donaldson, Scott. *Fool for Love: F. Scott Fitzgerald*. New York: Congdon and Weed, 1983.

Fitzgerald, F. Scott. *Afternoon of an Author: A Selection of Uncollected Stories and Essays*. Edited by Arthur Mizener. Princeton: Princeton UP, 1978.

———. *F. Scott Fitzgerald's Ledger: A Facsimile*. Washington, DC: NCR/Microcard, 1973.

———. *The Price Was High: The Last Uncollected Stories of F. Scott Fitzgerald*. Edited by

Matthew J. Bruccoli. New York: Harcourt Brace Jovanovich, 1979.

Grenberg, Bruce L. "Fitzgerald's 'Crack-Up' Essays Revisited: Fictions of the Self, Mirrors for a Nation." *F. Scott Fitzgerald: New Perspectives.* Edited by Jackson R. Bryer, Alan Margolies, and Ruth Prigozy. Athens: U of Georgia P, 2000. 203-15.

Guthrie [Hearne], Laura. Journal, summer of 1935. F. Scott Fitzgerald Additional Papers, Princeton University Library.

Kuehl, John, and Jackson R. Bryer, eds. *Dear Scott / Dear Max: The Fitzgerald-Perkins Correspondence.* New York: Scribner, 1971.

Mellow, James R. *Invented Lives: F. Scott and Zelda Fitzgerald.* Boston: Houghton Mifflin, 1984.

Meyers, Jeffrey. *Scott Fitzgerald: A Biography.* New York: HarperCollins, 1994.

Potts, Stephen W. *The Price of Paradise: The Magazine Career of F. Scott Fitzgerald.* San Bernardino: Borgo, 1993.

Reynolds, Michael. *Hemingway: The 1930s.* New York: Norton, 1997.

Wilson, Edmund, ed. *The Crack-Up.* New York: New Directions, 1945.

INDEX